INDUSTRIAL GWYNEDD

GWYNEDD DIWYDIANNOL

Cyfrol/Volume 2 : 1997

Editor/golygydd:

Dr David Gwyn

Gwynedd Archaeological Trust/Ymddiriedolaeth Archaeolegol Gwynedd

Editorial board/bwrdd golygyddol:

Griff Jones
Cae Clyd, Blaenau Ffestiniog

Dr Michael Lewis
Department of Adult and Continuing Education, University of Hull

Dr Gwynfor Pierce Jones
Pen y Groes

Gareth Haulfryn Williams, MA, DAA, JP
Assistant Director: Culture, Gwynedd County Council/Cyfarwyddwr Cynorthwyol: Diwylliant, Cyngor Sir Gwynedd

Andrew Davidson, BA
Gwynedd Archaeological Trust/Ymddiriedolaeth Archaeolegol Gwynedd

Notes on the contributors/nodiadau ar y cyfrannwyr:

Y mae Henry Williams wedi cymeryd diddordeb mawr yn archaeoleg a hanes diwydiannol Gogledd-orllewin Cymru ers blynyddoedd, ac y mae ef yn aelod Fforwm Plas Tan y Bwlch.

Dr John Llywelyn Williams lectures in the Department of Continuing Education at the University of Wales, Bangor, and is Warden of Neuadd John Morris Jones. A native of Bethesda, he has for a long time been fascinated by W. J. Parry's business activities.

Andrew Neale is a publisher and writer on industrial railway matters, and also runs a railway book business.

Gareth Haulfryn Williams is Assistant Director: Culture, Gwynedd County Council.

Dr Pam Michael lectures in the School of Community, Regional and Communication Studies at UWB, and previously worked on a research project examining the records of the North Wales Lunatic Asylum, which closed down in 1994. The article which appears below is based on a lecture given to a Gwynedd Archaeological Trust Day-School, *Y Chwarel a'i Phobl* (The Quarry and its People).

Distributed by Plateway Press, Taverner House, East Harling, Norfolk

Designed and printed by Postprint, East Harling, Norfolk

ISBN 1 871980 36 4

Contents/Cynnwys

Abbreviations/talfyriadau

The following abbreviations are standard:

Arch. Camb.: *Archaeologia Cambrensis*
BL: British Library, Russell Square, London
CCHChSF: *Cylchgrawn Cymdeithas Hanes a Chofnodion Sir Feirionydd*
CLlGC: *Cylchgrawn Llyfrgell Genedlaethol Cymru*
CRO: Caernarfon Record Office, Victoria Dock, Caernarfon, Gwynedd
DRO: Dolgellau Record Office, Dolgellau, Gwynedd
GAG: Gwasanaeth Archifau Gwynedd
GAS: Gwynedd Archives Service
JMHRS: *Journal of the Merionethshire Historical and Record Society*
LlGC: Llyfrgell Genedlaethol Cymru, Aberystwyth
LlRO: Llangefni Record Office, Shire Hall, Llangefni, Ynys Môn
NLW: National Library of Wales, Aberystwyth
NLWJ: *National Library of Wales Journal*
PCB: Prifysgol Cymru, Bangor
PRO: Public Record Office, Kew/Chancery Lane, London
TAAS: *Transactions of the Anglesey Antiquarian Society*
TCHS: *Transactions of the Caernarvonshire Historical Society*
TCHNM: *Trafodion Cymdeithas Hynafiaethwyr a Naturiaethwyr Môn*
TCHSG: *Trafodion Cymdeithas Hanes Sir Gaernarfon*
UWB: University of Wales, Bangor

Front cover: Two quarrymen reducing a slate slab with the rhys; from Morgan Richards' *Slate Quarrying and How to Make it Profitable.*

Awdur Chwareli Llechi Gogledd Cymru yn 1873

gan Henry Williams

Yn ystod chwarter olaf y bedwaredd ganrif ar bymtheg, yr oedd chwareli Gogledd Cymru yn eu hanterth a'r breuddwyd yn bodoli mai dal i gynyddu a wnaent, er gwaethaf ambell i igian hwyrach. O gofio bod cyfran helaeth o weithwyr tair sir a'u teuluoedd yn derbyn eu bara beunyddiol o'r diwydiant hwn, nid rhyfedd bod dyfodol y chwareli o ddiddordeb neilltuol i'r boblogaeth hon yn gyffredinol. Yn nechreu 1873, llwyddodd y *Carnarvon and Denbigh Herald* i gyflogi arbennigwr i ymweld â ardaloedd y chwareli ac ysgrifennu cyfres o erthyglau ar y diwydiant o ddiddordeb cyffredinol i'r darllenwyr. Penderfynodd yr *Herald* gyfieithu'r erthyglau hyn i'r Gymraeg a'u cyhoeddi, ychydig wythnosau ar ol y gwreiddiol, yn yr *Herald Gymraeg*. Ni ddatgelodd yr *Herald* enw'r gohebydd arbennig hwn o gwbl ac hyd heddiw nid oes sicrwydd pendant pwy oedd.

Yn ail hanner y ganrif hon mae'r diddordeb yn hanes y chwareli llechi wedi cynyddu yn enfawr, gyda chyhoeddi nifer o lyfrau ar wahanol agweddau o'r pwnc. Ymchwiliwr amlwg yn y maes yw'r Dr M.J.T. Lewis o Brifysgol Hull. Penderfynodd ef gasglu at ei gilydd yr oll o'r erthyglau uchod, yn y Saesneg gwreiddiol. Nid tasg fechan syml oedd y casglu, gan nad oes yn bodoli yn yr un o'r archifdai a llyfrgelloedd prifysgol yn y wlad gyfres gyflawn o'r ddwy *Herald*. Ond rhyngddynt oll, llwyddodd Dr Lewis i gael casgliad gweddol gyflawn o'r erthyglau a gyda chydweithrediad Canolfan Addysg y Parc Cenedlaethol ym Mhlas Tan y Bwlch, fe'i cyhoeddwyd yn 1987 dan y teitl *The Slate Quarries of North Wales in 1873*. Yn yr ysgrif agoriadol i'r llyfr, mae'r Dr Lewis yn trafod pwy allasai awdur yr erthyglau fod. Mae'n ystyried amryw o bosibiliadau amlwg, ond yn dod i'r casgliad nad yw'n bosibl mwyach penderfynnu pwy oedd yr awdur.

He was a Welsh-speaking Welshman, apparently a resident of Caernarfon, but certainly not directly involved in the industry. Nonetheless, he was a practical man, and one of his asides suggests that he might have been an architect or a builder. Middle-class, but not so grossly condescending as some in his attitude to the working man, he was adept enough in English to attempt, though not fully to succeed in, the verbose and flowery journalistic style of the period, and well enough educated to adorn it with foreign phrases and references to Shakespeare and Dickens.[1]

Gall unrhyw ddarllenydd sydd yn weddol gyfarwydd â daearyddiaeth y tair sir, ddilyn yn fanwl deithiau'r gohebydd arbennig a nodi, nid yn unig y chwareli lle y bu ond hefyd sylwi y chwareli hynny yr aeth heibio iddynt. Ceir yr argraff cryf na fu trwy giatiau chwareli y Penrhyn na Dinorwic pan yn ysgrifennu'r erthyglau ond gallasai bod wedi ymweld â chwarel Dinorwic mewn cyfnod cynnarach. Yr hyn a geir am y ddwy chwarel yma yw'r hyn oedd yn wybodaeth cyffredinol i chwarelwyr y cyfnod.[2] Sylwir hefyd, pan yn ymweld ac ardal Dolwyddelan, iddo wneud mor a mynydd o un chwarel ac anwybyddu yn llwyr rhai eraill.[3]

Ceir yr argraff hefyd fod gwybodaeth fanwl y gohebydd o'r gwahanol ardaloedd yn amrywio yn enfawr. O'i ymweliad â Blaenau Ffestiniog, gellir sylwi ei fod yn gyfarwydd a'r ardal ond heb fod yn enedigol ohonni.[4] Y mae'r un peth yn wir am Ddolwyddelan.[5]

Pan yn ysgrifennu am Ddyffryn Nantlle, dengys mân bethau nad oedd yn frodyr ohonni, ond ei fod yn gyfarwydd iawn â hi.[6] Mae fwy neu lai yn cyfaddef mal ymwelydd anfynych oedd i ardaloedd Abergynolwyn a Chorris.[7] Nid yw ei erthygl ar ardal Penmachno yn faith, ond ynddi

[1] Anhysb., *The Slate Quarries of North Wales in 1873*, gol. Dr M. J. T. Lewis (Penrhyndeudraeth 1987).
[2] *Herald Cymraeg*, 16 Mai 1873, t. 6, col. b–c, 23 Mai 1873, t. 6, col. a–c.
[3] *Herald Cymraeg*, 21 Mawrth 1873, t. 6, col. c.
[4] *Ibid*., 21 Chwefror 1873, t. 6, col. c–d, 28 Chwefror 1873, t. 6, col. b–d.
[5] *Ibid*., 21 Mawrth 1873, t.6, col. c.
[6] *Ibid*., 11 Ebrill 1873, t. 6, col. b–c, 18 Ebrill 1873, t. 6, col. c–d, 25 Ebrill 1873, t. 6, col. b–c, 16 Mai 1873, t. 6, col. b–c.
[7] *Ibid*., 21 Mawrth 1873, t. 6, col. c–d.

dengys wybodaeth o'r ardal a'i chymeriadau y buasai yn annodd i un nad oedd yn frodor fod yn berchenog ohonno o gwbl. Ceir yma y math o fanylion nad ymddangosant yn yr un o'r erthyglau eraill.

> Y mae Penmachno, hyd yn nod yn yr amserau diweddar hyn .... yn parhau i fod yn bentref henddull, afreolaidd, fel yr hen bentrefi Cymreig. Y trigolion ydynt fel un teulu mawr. Y mae pawb yn gydnabyddus a phawb arall, a chyfarcha y naill y llall gydag enw a chyfenw plaen, heb ddysgu yr arferiad diweddar o Feistrio eu gilydd.[8]

Ond wedi darllen yr erthyglau, cefais fy hunan mewn sefyllfa unigryw. Bum ers degau o flynyddoedd yn dioddef o'r salwch hwnnw sydd yn mynd i waed dyn, sef hel achau. Bellach mae gennyf wybodaeth helaeth iawn o'm cyndeidiau a'u perthnasau. Yn eu mysg mae mwy nac un fu'n amlwg yn hanes chwarelyddiaeth Gogledd Cymru. O'r rhai hyn yr oedd un, nid yn unig yn arbennigwr ar chwareli, ond hefyd yn awdur llyfr neu ddau. Mae'r llyfrau rheini allan o brint ers llawer dydd ond llwyddais i gael un i'm dwylo a'i ddarllen yn fanwl gyda chrym diddordeb (fel y gellid disgwyl). Nid yw'n syndod o gwbl felly, wrth imi ddarllen *The Slate Quarries of North Wales in 1873* fod gennyf syniad pur bendant pwy oedd awdur yr erthyglau. 'Roedd arddull ei ysgrifennu yn debyg iawn i'r llyfr a ddarllenais.[9] 'Roedd yr hyn a wyddwn o'i hanes yn ffitio i'r dim i'r sylwadau uchod o'i wybodaeth o wahanol ardaloedd. Yn ben ar y cwbl mae ei erthygl ar chwarel Bryn Eglwys, Abergynolwyn, yn datguddio'n bendant pwy oedd, tra mae'r erthygl ar Ddolwyddelan yn gymorth i gadarnhau hynny.

Ni fum eriod fawr nes na phentref Abergynolwyn i chwarel Bryn Eglwys, ac i bwrpas ymchwil hanesyddol, dibwynt hollol fuasai mynd yno heddiw. Mae'r lle wedi dadfeilio a newid cymaint fel nad yw yr hyn sydd weledwy yn golygu dim. Ond ceir darlun clir iawn o'r chwarel mewn llyfr gan Alan Holmes, *Slates from Abergynolwyn*.[10] Teithiau un diwrnod a wnaeth y gohebydd arbennig nes mynd i Abergynolwyn. Yno newidiodd y patrwm ac aros tros y penwythnos. Ni ddywed ble yr arhosodd, ond o ddarllen llyfr Alan Holmes deuir i'r casgliad, am amryw o resymau, nad oedd ond un lle iddo aros, a hynny yn nhy y prif oruchwyliwr. Y Prif Oruchwyliwr ar y pryd oedd Robert Williams (Cae Engan, Llanllyfni). Mae'n annodd credu y

buasai unrhyw ohebydd y *Caernarvon and Denbigh Herald* yn cael croeso tros y Sul yn nhy y Prif Oruchwyliwr, ond yr oedd un person fuasai wedi cael pob croeso felly gan Robert Williams. Y person hwnnw yn neb llai na Morgan Richards, Bangor.

Brodor o Benmachno oedd Morgan Richards, "Morgrugyn Machno"; ganwyd ef yng Nglan y Pwll yn y flwyddyn 1829, mab i Thomas Richards, chwarelwr, ac i Elinor, ei wraig. Symudodd i Fangor yn ei ieuenctid, a dechreuodd ei yrfa fel ysgolfeistr wyrcws Undeb Bangor a Beaumaris. Gweithiodd wedyn fel clerc a beili llys sirol hyd at ei ymddeoliad. Y mae cyfrifiad 1851 yn ei gofnodi yn byw yn Sgwar Britannia, Bangor, ond trigodd am flynyddoedd yn 306 Stryd Fawr, lle cadwodd ei wraig siop wlân. Fel aelod Bwrdd Iechyd Bangor, enillodd ef enw o fod un o radicaliaid y ddinas,[11] ac yn 1874 dewiswyd ef yn Llywydd cyntaf Undeb Chwarelwyr Gogledd Cymru am rhai misoedd, cyn i John Lloyd Jones, cyn-gyfarwyddwr cwmniau llechi, gymeryd y swydd.[12]

Mae'n fwy na thebyg fod Williams a Richards yn gyfeillion clos, wedi troi yn yr un diwydiant a masnach am flynyddoedd. Ond mwy na hynny, 'roedd tad Robert Williams yn gefnder cyfan i nain Morgan Richards o ochr ei dad. Cyn diwedd y ganrif, ysgrifennodd Robert Williams erthygl ar hanes ei deulu.[13] Ynddi mae'n sôn am gyfneither ei dad a'i ddisgrifiad ohonni yw nain Morgan Richards, Bangor, fel pe dylasai pob darllenydd wybod pwy oedd hwnnw ac nad oedd yr un o liaws o wyr a wyresau eraill o bwys o gwbl.

Mae'r disgrifiad o'r Ysgol Sul yn y chwarel yn ffitio Morgan Richards i'r dim.

> ... a chan fod Ysgol Sabbothol fechan yn cael ei chynnal yn y "llustai" yr hon a fynychir gan ychydig o'r rhai a breswyliasant yn nghymdogaeth y chwarel, treiliais fyr amser yno hytrach na phererindoda yn mhellach i chwilio am le addoliad. Yr oedd popbeth o gylch yr ysgol hon yn berfaith Gymraeg a chwbl wladaidd, ac adgofiai i mi gyfarfodydd yr Anghydffurfwyr cyn i Ddeddf Goddefiad fod yn achlysur i gannoedd o dai addoliad gael eu codi yn mhob parth o'r wlad ... Arweiniwyd fi i ddosbarth oedd dan ofal hen Buritan da. Yr oedd efe yn hyddysg mewn materion Ysgrythol, ac yr oeddym yn bur agos a dyfod yn gyfeillion, pan y

---

8 *Ibid.*, 21 Mawrth 1873, t. 6, col. b.
9 Morgan Richards, *Slate Quarrying and How to Make it Profitable* (London; Watts and Co., Bangor; Evan Williams, 1881).
10 Alan Holmes *Slates from Abergynolwyn* (Caernarfon 1986).
11 Peter Ellis Jones, *Bangor Local Board of Health, 1850–1883* (t.s. yn llyfrgell Bangor) tt. 18–19.
12 R. Merfyn Jones, *The Slate Quarrymen of North Wales 1874–1922* (Caerdydd: Gwasg Prifysgol Cymru, 1981) t. 135n.
13 Robert Williams, "Hunangofiant Chwarelwr, Rhan 1, Bore Oes Chwarelwr 1813–1839" *Cymru* cyf. XIX Gorff– Rhag 1900 t. 155 a 206. Gw. hefyd cyf. XVI rhif 90 Ionawr 15fed, tt. 55–9.

darfu i mi heb yn wybod daflu dwfr oer ar ein hymddyddan trwy ddyweud fy mod yn meddwl nad oedd yr efengylwr Matthew yn deall ond ychydig os dim am seryddiaeth, yr hyn oedd yn bur groes i syniadau yr hen gyfaill teilwng mewn perthynas i'r ffordd weddus o siarad yn ngylch yr apostol.[14]

O ddarllen *Hanes Methodistiaeth Arfon*, cawn i Richards fod yn selog iawn i grefydd a'r gyfundeb yn ei ieuenctid, ond iddo gilio yn raddol tros y blynyddoedd.[15] Ni wyddom i sicrwydd pa mor bell aeth y cilio erbyn 1873, ond y darlun a gawn o ddarllen hanes yr Ysgol Sul honno yw un o Morgan Richards yn arwynebol ymddangos ei fod yn cymeryd diddordeb yn y wers ond mewn gwirionedd yn brysur ddadanasodi pob person, yn blant a rhai hyn yn y lle – yr hun fuasai'n nodweddiadol ohonno.

Yn ei erthygl ar Ddolwyddelan, mae gohebydd yr *Herald* yn canmol i'r cymylau chwarel newydd Owain Gethin Jones yr adeiladydd, ac yn llwyo anwybyddu chwareli eraill yr ardal, oedd yn fwy chwareli ac yn cynyrchu mwy: "Ychydig o ddynion sydd yma yn gweithio hyd yn hyn, ond ar agwedd a rhagolygon Chwarel Gethin y dymunwn wneud sylw byr ..."[16]

Os mai Morgan Richards yw'r gohebydd neilltuol, mae hyn yn hollol dealladwy, gan fod Gethin yn ffrind personol ac agos i deulu Morgan Richards. Hyd y gwyddom, nid oedd perthynas gwaed, ond 'roedd y cyfeillgarwch yn ddigon clos i Gethin gyfansoddi cyfres o ddwsin o englynion coffa i fam Morgan Richards[17] a hanner dwsin o englynion llongyfarch i Thomas, brawd Morgan Richards, ar ei briodas.[18]

Os mai Morgan Richards yw'r gohebydd arbennig, hawdd deall na fu yn chwareli Dinorwig a Phenrhyn. 'Roedd yn hollol anerbyniol yng Nghastell y Penrhyn oherwydd materion llywodraeth a pholitics lleol Bangor ac yn nes ymlaen yn anerbyniol hollol gan stâd y Vaenol, oherwydd materion chwarelyddiaeth.

Tra nad yw'r hyn oll yn profi tu draw i amheuaeth mai Morgan Richards oedd gohebydd arbennig yr *Herald*, yr wyf wedi'm llwyr argyhoeddi mai ef oedd yr ysgrifenydd. Dylwn hwyrach ychwanegu, er nad yw Robert Williams, Morgan Richards na minnau yn disgyn yn uniongyrchol naill o'r llall, mae'r tri ohonom yn disgyn o Thomas Morgan a'i wraig Ellen Francis, a fagodd deulu yn Nantlle, ynghanol y ddeunawfed ganrif.

In this article Mr Williams discusses the authorship of the anonymous series of articles on slate quarries which appeared in the Caernarvon and Denbigh Herald *and in the* Herald Cymraeg *in 1873, and which were printed as a booklet by the Snowdonia National Park in 1987, edited by Dr Michael Lewis. He argues that the author was Morgan Richards of Bangor, "Morgrugyn Machno", on the evidence of the author's familiarity with certain places and not with others, on the praise he bestows on a known friend's quarry, and the sceptical approach to Christianity he demonstrates.*

---

[14] *Herald Cymraeg* 21 Mawrth 1873, t. 6, col. c–d.

[15] William Hobley, *Hanes Methodistiaeth Arfon cyf. 6, Dosbarth Bangor* (Cyfarfod Misol Arfon, 1924) t. 127; pennod ar gapel y Tabernacl M.C. Bangor. Gw. hefyd t. 328.

[16] *Herald Cymraeg* 21 Mawrth 1873, t. 6, col. b.

[17] "Ellen Richards. Gwraig Mr. Thomas Richards, Manchester House, Penmachno, mam y Meistri Morgan a Thos. Richards, Bangor ...."*Gweithiau Gethin* (W. J. Robert, Llanrwst 1884) t. 57.

[18] *Ibid.*, t. 75

Two Powder Magazines in the Parish of Llanllechid, Bethesda:

their significance in the industrial turmoil of the late Nineteenth Century

by Dr John Llywelyn Williams

Explosives magazines are distinctive if unspectacular industrial monuments. The two powder magazines erected by W. J. Parry formed part of his trading concerns, one, at Cilfoden near Bethesda, erected after it became clear that it was unsafe to store explosives in the town of Bethesda itself, the other, at Hafoty, erected and used temporarily after he lost control of the Cilfoden site. The commercial and political implications of his supplying Penrhyn Quarries with explosives whilst supporting the Quarrymen's Union are discussed here.

1. Introduction

The varied and often unique industrial monuments of the slate quarries of Gwynedd have attracted much attention from historians and industrial archaeologists alike during the last decade, particularly since many of the abandoned quarries have now become derelict, whilst modern planning schemes have led to the total removal of some of the enterprises. This article has been prompted by two powder magazines, buildings that command a lowly status in the hierarchy of industrial monuments, that are to be found in the parish of Llanllechid on the north-eastern outskirts of the slate quarrying town of Bethesda, Gwynedd.

In themselves powder magazines are not spectacular monuments to be distinguished as a class by outstanding design or architecture, but rather represent utilitarian structures built for the purpose of storing the explosive requirements of their particular extractive industry — in the present context, slate quarrying. Powder magazines were licensed structures which had to conform to the legal requirements laid down in the Gunpowder Act of 1860 and the Explosives Act of 1875. This required that such buildings be solidly built and protected with walls of a particular thickness; that the inside be thoroughly dry, which necessitated the lining of the inner walls with wooden planking thus creating an enclosed inner tinder dry chamber; and finally, that the explosives had to be separately stored from the detonators, which therefore required the building of small extensions to house the latter. Powder magazines were to be open for inspection and were licensed to store only prescribed amounts of explosive materials. Usually magazines would be sited within close proximity and convenience to the source of extraction of its prescribed industry.

2. Structural details of the two magazines

The two powder magazines which are the subject of this article stand today as badly ruined structures within their upland locations (Fig. 1). They are not, however, without features of interest arising from their isolated position, their size and their structural details. Both magazines were built within a distance of about half a mile of each other, far removed from any quarry or excavation with which they might have been associated. The two magazines were located on the Cefnfaes Estate, a small private enclave which is almost totally surrounded by the estate of Lord Penrhyn, the owner of the massive quarry which bore his name in the adjoining parish of Llandygai, though it abuts on unenclosed Crown land on the open mountain side.

The structural details of the two buildings are presented below:

a) The Cilfoden Magazine (SH 6283 6725) (Fig. 2).

A plan of this building exists in the *Inventory of the Royal Commission on Ancient Monuments for Caernarfonshire*[1] but does not show any details of the inner partitioning of the structure into two rooms. The magazine

---

[1] *Royal Commission on Ancient and Historic Monuments (Wales) Caernarvonshire vol. 1 East* (H.M.S.O. 1956), fig. 135.

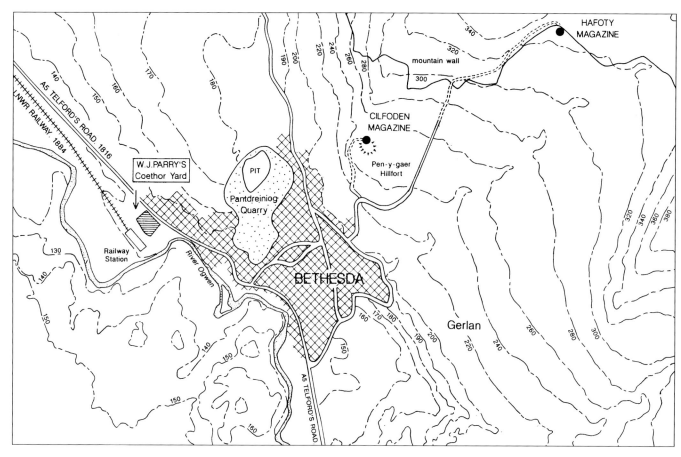

Fig 1 *The location of W. J. Parry's two powder magazines.*

was built on the immediate northern perimeter of the prehistoric hillfort of Pen y Gaer which surmounts a small hillock at approximately 260 metres (850 feet) above O.D. The site commands an imposing view across the Ogwen Valley and the red door of the magazine was a well known landmark in the district until the building was abandoned and began to disintegrate from the 1960s onwards. The structure consists of an inner chamber approximately 8m x 3.7m in ground plan, surrounded by an outer enclosure wall 12m x 8m in size and entered at its eastern end by a 2m x 3m portico-like vestibule. The main chamber was divided into two rooms, the inner length of the eastern room being 3.30m, the western 1.50m and both were separated by a 90cm baffled void between 65cm thick walls. The rooms were entered through separate doors placed at either end of the building. The walls of the explosives chamber were built of mortared local undressed stone and includes some brickwork around the eastern entrance. No window openings were provided in the 65cm thick walls. The chamber walls still stand to a height of approximately 2.4m on the northern side but the building is now roofless, the original slates of the pitched roof having been long

removed. The building is disintegrating rapidly, a process aided by the slipshod manner in which it seems to have been erected. Access was along a rough farm track which negotiated the western steep flank of the hill from the yard of Cilfoden Farm. The magazine was built in 1899 and last used for explosive storage in 1949 by the son of the original owner.

b) Hafoty magazine (also known as Foty Bach and the site was referred to by a much older generation of Llanllechid farmers as Beudy Newydd) (SH636276773) (Fig. 3).

The magazine is built on the lower slopes of Moel Faban on the junction with the marshy floor of the upper reaches of Afon Ffrydlas in the shallow valley called Gweuncwysmai. The approximate height is 300m above O.D. and the building stands inside the boundary wall of the Cefnfaes estate with the unenclosed mountain. It is a lonely and desolate spot far away from any surrounding habitation and consequently remote of access. The building is a very imposing structure, measuring approximately 7.27m in length by 4.75m in width and built of undressed boulders and stone, and though today roofless, still stands

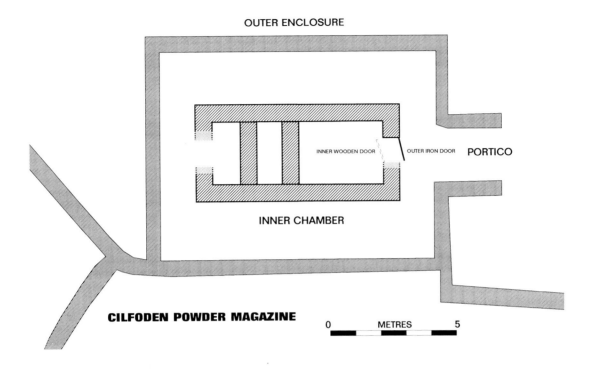

Fig 2 *Cilfoden powder magazine.*

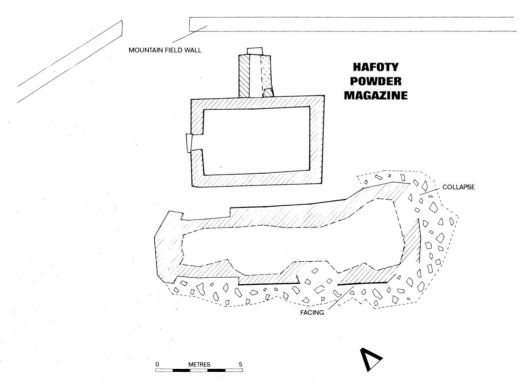

Fig 3 *Hafoty powder magazine.*

to a height immediately below the eaves of approximately 2.5m on the upper north side and 3m on the south. The walls are 53cm thick, windowless and with a north facing entrance door. Four small air vents have been positioned in each corner at a level above the suspended floor. On the east side stands a badly ruined lean-to annex with its own outside entrance; the chamber of this small annex measured 1.8m x 2.3m overall. There is no evidence of the original roofing structure of the building but a pitched slated roof is attested by the angle of the one remaining gable and the few smashed slates still littering the adjoining ground surface. The building has been erected on a sloping uneven surface with the ground falling quite sharply to the south. Thus the floor in the southern part of the building stands on a plinth some 85cm high, and in consequence the floor would have been of a suspended wooden type. Originally the inside of the chamber would have been built like a large tinder dry wooden cupboard with the walls and ceiling lined with timber cladding, but none of this timbering is evident today.

One of the most notable features of the magazine is the huge, slightly crescent-shaped stone revetted earthen and boulder bank which extends along and beyond the whole outer length of the western side of the magazine. This is a most imposing structure measuring approximately 13m long by 5m wide and still standing to a height of 2m. It presumably represents an elaborate protective muffle to the building in case of an explosion, although it is debatable whether the bank, with its plentiful stone and boulder content, would have served as a greater hazard under such circumstances. The fact that this bank is not continued on the eastern side would suggest that it may be an older structure, alongside or into which the magazine had been inserted. In this context the original name for the site, Beudy Newydd ("new cowshed"), may suggest that it had replaced an earlier structure on site, although the present configuration of the mound may have concealed or even destroyed such evidence, if it had ever existed in the first place. The magazine was built in 1903 and was in use for only a brief period of time, partly because of its inaccessibility but largely because of commercial reasons to be investigated shortly, before being abandoned and left slowly to disintegrate.

3. The historical significance of the powder magazines

Although the architectural details of the magazines are of some interest, they assume greater importance in the context of the socio-political history of Bethesda. Their significance is to be measured in the context of the industrial turmoil that engulfed the slate quarrying community of the Ogwen Valley in the latter part of the nineteenth century and culminated in the disastrous three-year Penrhyn lock-out of 1900–1903. The buildings in question thus become the mute witnesses to these events and to the public and personal rivalries that raged between the two principal proponents, Lord Penrhyn and William John Parry.

Much of the information documented below is contained in the series of Letter Books that Parry left as part of his personal archive to the University of Wales, Bangor, and the National Library of Wales, Aberystwyth. Various aspects of their content, particularly Parry's involvement with the explosives trade, have been discussed elsewhere.[2]

The two powder magazines were built for the local business man and entrepreneur W. J. Parry who played a leading political role in the slate quarrying communities of Gwynedd within the last decades of the nineteenth century. Parry was one of the founding fathers of the North Wales Quarrymen's Union in 1874 and had striven valiantly to gain political and economic recognition for its workforce. W. J. Parry was also one of the trustees of the Cefnfaes estate upon which the village of Bethesda had been built from the 1820s onwards, the village growing and jostling for space with a small, independently owned slate quarry by the name of Pantdreiniog. Parry had been instrumental in the development of this quarry since about 1890 and had been briefly its general manager in 1897. (All vestiges of this quarry were removed in a Welsh Office landscape reclamation scheme which dated to the 1960s).

But the economic life of the Ogwen valley was dominated by the massive industrial enterprise of the Penrhyn Quarry which, from humble beginnings in the eighteenth century, had developed to become one of the largest integrated slate quarries in the world. By the last decades of the century the owner of that concern was the second Baron Penrhyn, George Sholto Gordon Douglas Pennant and, in the course of his austere supremacy, he fought with Parry an acrimonious and vindictive political battle in public that culminated in the events leading to,

2   J. Ll. Williams, "Political Victimisation in Late Nineteenth Century Gwynedd: the case of W. J. Parry" *Llafur* vol. 7, pp. 41-52

and arising from, the great Penrhyn strike of 1900–1903. Privately, they were also locked in a most revengeful personal conflict, and the two powder magazines came to represent the public image of that inner conflict between two determined and ruthless rivals.

One important facet of Parry's many commercial interests was his flourishing business as a General Merchant in Bethesda. He had established his firm in 1862 and his yard was situated on the southern edge of the village on premises that he later, and most conveniently, came to share with the railway station and goods yard. He sold every manner of commercial product ranging from ironmongery to household furniture but concentrated on bulk industrial products such as oil, cement, coal, lime and, most important of all, gunpowder and explosives. His trade in the latter was probably the cornerstone of his commercial interests and his clients included most of the major quarries, mines and industrial enterprises in north west Gwynedd and Anglesey. From 1877 Parry had held the coveted and highly lucrative agency of the Nobel Powder Company in his area. The Penrhyn Quarry was one of Parry's principal clients and this trade alone ensured an annual sale of several tons of gunpowder, as well as the quarry's gelignite, detonators, fuses, cartridges and caps. (In 1886, to take one year at random, it is roughly estimated that Penrhyn sold 129,945 pounds of powder to the quarrymen and this would have been purchased through Parry's agency.)[3]

In 1892 Parry lost the Penrhyn order and this triggered a calamitous chain of events that blighted Parry and his business enterprises for the remaining decade of the century and culminated with Lord Penrhyn adding a bankruptcy petition as part of his famous libel action against Parry in 1903. The order was withdrawn from him as part of a highly orchestrated punitive campaign waged by the Penrhyn dynasty against Parry. He was being punished for his general anti-management, pro-Quarryman's Union activities, but, more specifically for submitting crucial and devastating evidence against the Penrhyn regime before the Royal Commission on Labour on the state of the slate quarrying industry which had reported in London in 1892, a coincidence that was to be

Plate 1 *The Cilfoden powder magazine, on the left-hand side of the brow of the hill.* *Courtesy David Longley*

³ CRO: PQ13/1.

strongly denied later by the Penrhyn family as the cause for the withdrawal of the order.

The immediate effect of the withdrawal threatened to cause serious imbalances in the web of interrelated business enterprises which Parry had built up. The situation was made more precarious since Parry was heavily in debt to the bank, because, earlier in the century, he had obtained a loan of £1,000 to finance some undocumented business enterprise. His commercial position was further weakened when in October 1896 a devastating fire razed his commercial yard in Bethesda, causing him massive losses for which he was only partly insured. It was in this yard, although it was closely adjacent to a heavily populated part of the village, that Parry stored his gunpowder and explosives. Although, mercifully, there were no serious injuries or deaths resulting from what was a very serious conflagration, it was clear that in future Parry would have to seek a safer venue to store his explosive merchandise. This he sought temporarily in one of the magazines of the Pantdreiniog Quarry an arrangement that was to prove inadequate since the quarry did not belong to him and the magazine in question was only licensed to store gunpowder.

In January 1897 Parry first broached the matter of securing a new powder magazine with Nobel in a letter:

> I said long ago and repeatedly that I believe I could get my 10 Trustees of the Cefnfaes Estate to lease a piece of land on their estate for a magazine, but got no word to ask me to try and secure it. The trustees meet next month and I could lay the application before them then if you so wish.[4]

There followed a series of letters between the correspondents concerning details of the ultimate ownership of the site should Parry cease to be the Nobel representative in the area, before ultimately agreement was reached whereby Nobel agreed to bear the costs of building the new magazine on land leased from the Cefnfaes estate.

The location of the new magazine was to be at Carneddi, Bethesda, on the land of Cilfoden farm in the lee of the Pen y Gaer hillfort. Thus came to be built the Cilfoden magazine. Parry was fulsome in his praise of the site claiming that "it is within less than a mile of the Bethesda station" (he did not add, however, that the mile contained some of the steepest hills in the Bethesda neighbourhood and that the cartage fee for two tons of explosives from the Bethesda railway station was £2);[5] "that the spot is perfectly dry with a rock foundation and no danger of flooding and that the road can be made with very little expense good for all purposes."[6] He did, nevertheless, mention in a letter to Nobel dated 1 April 1898 that the field adjoining the site belonged to the Penrhyn Estate and that they should first ascertain whether there would be any opposition from that quarter. The matter lingered on until June when Parry was informed by the retiring Estate Agent that neither his successor nor Lord Penrhyn were likely to object to the siting of the magazine.[7] Plans and the official papers for the project were lodged with the County Council and the date for the hearing and appeal interregnums period fixed for 4 August and 22 September respectively. A Licensing Committee was also appointed and Parry informs Nobel that he was a member of this committee and had succeeded to get a majority of friends put on it. "Lord P. was at first inclined to object but I passed a short note explaining to him and got the enclosed in reply." (Unfortunately, his answer has not been appended to the letter.)[8] An objection, however, was to come from the most unlikely of quarters, namely the Local District Council, on the grounds that the magazine was to be registered in the wrong parish, Parry having inadvertently written Llanllechid instead of Bethesda in the application. This slip was to prove costly since the matter had to be referred to the Home Office who proposed that the meeting of the Licensing Committee be adjourned for a further six weeks. Eventually, the licence was granted on November 11 1898 but not before Parry had had the Chief Constable of the County, Colonel Ruck, to visit and pronounce on the suitability of the site.[9] The scheme was put out to tender a month later with eleven builders, from as far afield as Llandudno, Menai Bridge, Bangor and even Connah's Quay in Flintshire, being approached by Parry personally. Much to his disappointment, only two responded – "the situation of the building is against people tendering for it"[10] was Parry's reaction to the lack of interest – but eventually a bid was accepted and work was began during the first week of April 1899[11] after Parry had impressed upon the builder that the work had to be done in every respect in strict accordance with the Draft Licence and the plan and specifications.[12]

---

4   U.W.B. Coetmor MS 65 p. 650.
5   U.W.B. Coetmor MS, cartage account, June 1902.
6   U.W.B. Coetmor MS 65 p. 780, p. 909, p. 916.
7   U.W.B. Coetmor MS 68 p. 161.
8   U.W.B. Coetmor MS 68 p. 261.
9   U.W.B. Coetmor MS 68 p. 358, p. 359, p. 436, p. 469.
10   U.W.B. Coetmor MS 68 p. 626.
11   U.W.B. Coetmor MS 68 p. 823.
12   U.W.B. Coetmor MS 68 p. 775.

The name of the builder entrusted with the work is not known but his project took another five months to complete, the protracted building period being accounted for by inclement weather and, of all things in the heart of the world's most important slate belt, a lack of roofing slates.[13] The keys were finally handed to Parry on 10 August 1899,[14] the whole marathon having taken, from its agitated inception to its completion, a total of nineteen weary months.

The loss of the prestigious Penrhyn explosives order had always been a matter of great concern to the Nobel company. As early as 1892 they had expressed their dissatisfaction with Parry and it was evident that they were allowing some of their products to enter the Penrhyn Quarry by various devious means and without consultation with him. They were also engaged in a policy of destabilising Parry by forcing him to maintain fixed prices with his clients whilst allowing others to negotiate lower rates for the same products. Parry was aware as early as 1895 that an "explosives ring"[15] was operating against him amongst the chief quarry proprietors and that a conspiracy of "Conservative owners"[16] could force him out of business. It therefore came as no surprise when he was abruptly informed by Nobel on May 7 1902 that his agency was to be terminated on the thirty-first of that same month.

Parry summarises the whole sorry episode in a letter written on 11 June 1902 to a Mr G. Smith of Falkirk, a business friend and a fellow agent:

Yes it was unfortunate that the connection was severed at last, but very natural, and I have no reason to complain. When the Penrhyn orders were first lost I wrote explaining all and offered to resign. Afterwards I was led to expect that they would come back. I hope that we can deal pleasantly together and to our natural advantages as Dealers together. As long as this can be done I shall not want to look to another source for my supplies, but naturally I shall try to keep well with my friends, who have patronised me, some of them for years before I was

Plate 2 *The Hafoty powder magazine.*   *Courtesy Nathan Yates*

[13] U.W.B. Coetmor MS 68 p. 899; 70 p. 152.
[14] U.W.B. Coetmor MS 70 p. 196.
[15] U.W.B. Coetmor MS 63 p. 177.
[16] U.W.B. Coetmor MS 66 p. 318.

connected with Nobels. This will be no loss to Nobels or their new agent here, as I shall be selling at their prices and the Agent will be getting his Commission and I shall only be getting my 5% as dealer and the cartage at the scale already agreed upon. Nothing can be fairer than this.[17]

On the 30 May immediately prior to his dismissal, the Cilfoden magazine carried the following stock of explosive materials, an indication basically of how well Parry managed his agency on behalf of Nobel.[18] His problem was that his successor had now the right to use the magazine.

Blasting gelignite	Gelatine dynamite	Gelignite	Quintuple detonators	Sextuples detonators	Octuples detonators
1000	2700	3600	2600	13000	500

Cable	Con.w.	RJ	Cylinder	Warming pans	Rippers
300ft	50ft	1 coil	1	7	6

Such a serious business setback did not, however, deter Parry. Through various influential friends such as Lloyd George, he sought, and eventually gained, the agency of the Birmingham-based Kynock Explosives Company for North Wales, Cheshire and Staffordshire. Immediately, as from 1 August,[19] he set himself the task of keeping his old and winning new clients within his greatly expanded territory. His policy was to "put a man on the ground as well as work it myself", a daunting task for a man in his sixty-first year. To one of his old clients, Captain Evans of the Trecastell Mine at Henryd, he wrote on 14 August:

The gelatin has been tested by Government and stands the test in every respect equal to Nobels. As you have seen no doubt the Government let their contract to Kynock. Workmen as you are aware take an unreasonable fancy when a new thing is introduced. The price is the same as you will see from the enclosed invoice – the first item being Nobels and the other Kynock.[20]

By 11 October Parry writes to Atkins, his principal managerial contact at Kynocks, and quotes from Captain Evans' reply – "I am satisfied with the stuff I get from you" and adds that he told Nobel's agent when he called that it was so.[21]

His endeavours on behalf of Kynock were obviously quite successful as his first statement of supplies from the company show:

Supplies

July 31	Explosives	£40. 5.0
Aug 6	Explosives	£ 4.12.9
Aug 13	Black Powder	£28.16.0
Aug 15	Explosives	£17.10.0
Aug 21	Black Powder	£30. 0.0
Sept 4	Explosives	£48.15.0
Sept 10	Explosives	£ 1.10.0 [22]

They indicate that his volume of trade had not diminished markedly in the transition period from one company to another and this is confirmed in the following extract from a letter of thanks addressed to William Evans of Birmingham, dated 16 October. Parry writes:

It is likely to be much better for me than the Agency for Nobels ever was. I have secured all their customers who I previously supplied except Darbishires who had a hand with Penrhyn to throw me off Nobels after representing them for upwards of 25 years.[23]

Doubtless the transition was assisted by the fact that Parry had at least access to Nobel products, as his agreement with Smith of Falkirk indicated in the previously quoted letter, although there is no indication in the Letter Books that he used this contact to his advantage. By November such was his expanding business success that Parry was in a position to offer an appointment to a business colleague by the name of William Hughes from Chester as a sub-agent for Shropshire, Cheshire and Staffordshire.[24]

When Parry had first thought of obtaining the Kynock agency the concept of a powder magazine had been central to his strategy, as the following extract from a letter to William George, his solicitor, shows. It is dated 31 May. He writes:

Is your brother [i.e. *David Lloyd George, M.P. for the Caernarfon Boroughs*] over? If he was at home on Wednesday or any day after Tuesday I would like to run over to see him, if he could not run over here for a few hours. My object is to try if he could not get at Kynock through Mr Wm Evans of Birmingham to secure their agency which is a powerful rival to Nobels and I know they want a site for a store in North Wales and I might get one for them on the Cefnfaes Estate.[25]

[17] U.W.B. Coetmor MS 78 p. 216.
[18] U.W.B. Coetmor MS 78 p. 195.
[19] U.W.B. Coetmor MS 78 p. 256.
[20] U.W.B. Coetmor MS 78 p. 270.
[21] U.W.B. Coetmor MS 78 p. 337.
[22] U.W.B. Coetmor MS 78 p. 411.
[23] U.W.B. Coetmor MS 78 p. 350.
[24] U.W.B. Coetmor MS 78 p. 350.
[25] U.W.B. Coetmor MS 78 p. 199.

THE PENRHYN LIBEL TRIAL.

SKETCHES AT YESTERDAY'S HEARING.

SPECIALLY DRAWN FOR THE "LIVERPOOL DAILY POST" AND "ECHO."

Mr YOUNG
THE QUARRY MANAGER

Mr W J PARRY
IN THE WITNESS BOX

1.—Interested Quarrymen.

2.—Mr. Robson to the Jury: "The issue of the case is the fact of Lord Penrhyn being in his attitude to his men a hard and unjust employer."

Plate 3a *The Penrhyn Libel Trial.*

1.—Lord Penrhyn is asked if he made any charge of dishonourable conduct against the men. 2.—Lord Penrhyn gives evidence in the body of the c
3.—Mr. Artemus Jones 4.—Mr. Robson, K.C., cross-examining Lord Penrhyn. 5.—Mr. Charles Mathews.

SKETCHES AT YESTERDAY'S HEARING.

SPECIALLY DRAWN FOR THE "DAILY POST" AND "ECHO."

Plate 3b *The Penrhyn Libel Trial.*

The subject of a new powder magazine in Bethesda had obviously been broached with the Kynock Company sometime before Parry wrote to Atkins on 20 September acknowledging their decision to build, and requesting details so that a plan could be submitted for approval to the Quarterly meeting of the County Council in the first week of November.[26]

Parry was eager for the work to start as soon as possible and even recommended that Atkins at Kynock send details to four local builders to tender for the contract, doubtless wishing not to repeat the embarrassing situation of the previous building programme when few tenders were received for the Cilfoden Magazine.[27] In order further to facilitate the passage of the application through the County Council he also advocated that notification of the proposed development be placed in three local newspapers which had representatives on the council, a ploy which he had successfully used with the Nobel application.[28] But to no avail, since the bureaucratic mills of the County Council ground very slowly. Thus the application, under the provision of the 1875 Explosives Act, for the erection of a magazine at Hafoty, Cilfoden, Bethesda, for the storage of mixed explosives, could not be heard before 12 March 1903 at Caernarfon.[29]

This day had particular significance for Parry since it coincided with the last day of the three day hearing of the Penrhyn libel action against him which was held in London (see plate 3). The outcome is well known, resulting in Lord Penrhyn's action being upheld by the court with total damages and costs being also held against Parry. The outcome of the Caernarfon application is not recorded in Parry's letter books or, to be more precise, the evidence has been removed since the pages for the period in question, all 174, have been deliberately ripped from the book.[30] The Kynock application must have been successful, for the magazine was built and still stands in its present ruined condition, but all the details relating to its erection and the reasons for building the earthen mound no longer exist in the Parry archive.

As a final postscript it should be added that Parry held an explosives agency until his death in 1927 although there are no references in his papers to the name of the company. The agency was then passed on to his son William who held it until his retirement when the last box of explosives was removed from the Cilfoden magazine in 1949. It would appear that Parry in the course of time and

at an unknown date must have regained the use of the Cilfoden magazine, thus making redundant the more solidly-built Hafoty building which was so difficult to reach and so impracticable within any business and commercial frame of reference.

The two powder magazines that have been the subject of this note are indeed minor industrial buildings. They are not without their passing interest, particularly the larger more intact Hafoty example, but the documentation attached to their building and the role that they played in the contorted labour history of the slate quarrying industry of the Ogwen Valley in the last decade of the nineteenth century, and culminating in the disastrous three year dispute of the Penrhyn Strike of 1900–03, belies their importance as simple industrial structures. Indeed the term "monument", within its connotation of a memorial or a commemoration, may be appropriately used to describe these two ruined buildings that bear silent witness to one of the most tragic and bitter breakdowns in industrial relations within the history of British labour politics, and the words "intrigue", "spite", "deception" and "revenge" have been inextricably enmeshed into their very fabric.

4. Acknowledgements

It is a pleasure to thank Mr Arnold Davies of Carneddi and Mr Emyr Roberts of Fferm Cilfoden for allowing access to visit both monuments; to Mr Ifor Williams of Fferm Coetmor for drawing the author's attention to the significance of the magazines – incidentally, his father was the principal haulier of gunpowder from the Bethesda L.N.W.R. station to the two sites, and Mr Williams himself assisted W. J. Parry's son to take the final box of gunpowder from the Cilfoden Magazine in 1949. In researching the subject the author has received gracious assistance from the respective staffs of the Gwynedd Archive Service at Caernarfon, the Archive of the National Library of Wales, Aberystwyth and particularly from Mr Tomos Roberts and Ms Diane Clarke in The Archives Department of the University of Wales, Bangor. The manuscript has been read and commented upon by Dr D. A. Jenkins, Mr Alwyn Roberts and Mr Tomos Roberts of the University of Wales, Bangor and through their kindness and judgment has been substantially improved. I am indebted to Mrs Nerys Hague for editing the final manuscript, and to Mr Roland Flook and Mr L. A. Dutton for surveying and drawing the two magazines.

---

[26] U.W.B. Coetmor MS 78 p. 312.
[27] U.W.B. Coetmor MS 78 p. 416.
[28] U.W.B. Coetmor MS 78 p. 407, p. 481.
[29] U.W.B. Coetmor MS 78 p. 481.
[30] U.W.B. Coetmor MS 78.

Broad Gauge at Holyhead

by Andrew Neale

Contrary to popular belief among railway historians, when the last broad gauge train on the Great Western Railway arrived at Paddington from Exeter on 20 May 1892, the Brunel gauge did not pass out of existence. A broad gauge locomotive remained in use at Holyhead for several more decades.

The building of the Chester and Holyhead Railway involved an improved harbour at Holyhead, with parliamentary approval being granted on 22 July 1847 for the construction of a lengthy breakwater, originally intended to be 5,360' long, but subsequently extended by a further 2,500'. This effectively doubled the capacity of the harbour.

The contract for this work was let on 24 December 1847 to Messrs J. and C. Rigby, a Westminster-based firm of contractors, with actual work commencing in January 1848. The large quantities of stone needed for this work were obtained by quarrying the adjoining Holyhead Mountain and laying nearly 2½ miles of railway to convey the stone to Soldier's Point, the start of the "Great Breakwater". A further extension from this point led to Salt Island, where a proposed east breakwater was to be built, though in the event this was never started and the rails were removed some time after 1853.[1] The line was a completely isolated system and was laid to the "broad" (7') gauge. This ensured stability in operation on a very

Plate 4 *Queen Victoria travels on the breakwater railway, 1853; from* The Illustrated London News. *Note that while her husband's train was locomotive-hauled, the Queen is horse-drawn – perhaps so the smuts will not spoil her dress?*

[1] D. Lloyd Hughes, Dorothy M. Williams, *Holyhead: The Story of a Port* (Denbigh, 1981) p. 91, pp. 94–5.

Plate 5 *A view of the quarries, showing hand and steam-cranes, and a locomotive with a full run about to depart for the breakwater; from* The Illustrated London News.

Plate 6 *The breakwater under construction, looking east; from* The Illustrated London News.

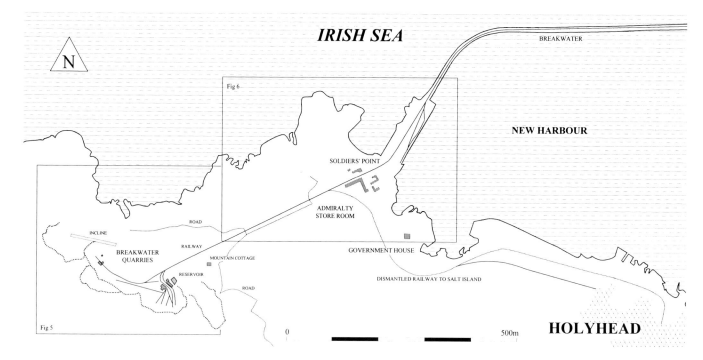

Fig 4 *Holyhead 7' gauge railway in 1900.*

exposed and windswept site, and was used on a number of other locomotive-worked breakwater and harbour railways, such as Portland in Dorset, the East London Harbour in South Africa, and in the Azores.[2]

The works were on a massive scale. In the quarries, explosions of gunpowder were set off by electric battery. Fifty moveable cranes, some steam-powered, were used, and at one point a counter-balance incline, whose trace can still be seen, brought stone down from the upper levels.

Rigby's engineer Rendel[3] devised a method whereby a timber staging "of five roads" (presumably five parallel tracks) 40' above water 150' wide was supported on piles 80' long. Loaded wagons made their way to Soldier's Point, initially by gravity, then tipped, discharging between eight and ten tons through staging. 5,000 tons a day could be tipped. Cranes on staging lifted the piles into position, which were then adjusted by small screw steam-vessel.

The returning empty wagons were initially horse-drawn; even after locomotives had arrived, fifty horses were employed.[4]

After four years, locomotives arrived to take over.[5] Six peculiar 0-4-0 well tank locomotives were built in 1852 by R. B. Longridge of Bedlington Ironworks, Northumbria. The two inside cylinders were of $10^{1}/_{4}$" bore by 18" stroke with steel-tyred Low Moor iron wheels of 3' 2" diameter on a wheelbase of 7' 6". The three well tanks held around 500 gallons of water and the boiler was of 3' diameter eighty $1^{3}/_{4}$" tubes 5' 5" in length. The firebox heating-surface was $32'^{2}$. The cylinders were mounted between the boiler and the frames.[6]

Plate 7 *An end-on view of the staging; from* The Illustrated London News.

[2]   See Alfred Rosling Bennett, *The Chronicles of Boulton's Siding* (Locomotive Publishing Company, 1927) p. 184, pp. 187–189 and Rowland A. S. Abbott, *Vertical Boiler Locomotives* (Oakwood Press, 1989) p. 41. The 7' gauge was used on a considerable number of locations where stability is essential. Many self-propelled rail cranes have been built either to 7' gauge or as dual-gauge with one set of wheels running on 4' $8^{1}/_{2}$ rails.

[3]   J. M. Rendel superintended the works until his death in 1856, when he was succeeded by John Hawkshaw. See *Illustrated London News,* vol. 63 23 August 1873 p. 179, col. c.

[4]   *Illustrated London News,* vol. 23 3 September 1853, p. 188 cols a–c; see also *Proceedings of the Institution of Civil Engineers,* 1876 pp. 95–130.

[5]   For details of the locomotives' arrival and departure, see V. J. Bradley, *Industrial Locomotives of North Wales* (Industrial Railway Society, 1992) pp. 289–292.

[6]   Alfred Rosling Bennett, *op. cit.,* pp. 183–189. See also *The Locomotive Magazine* 15 August 1905 p. 134.

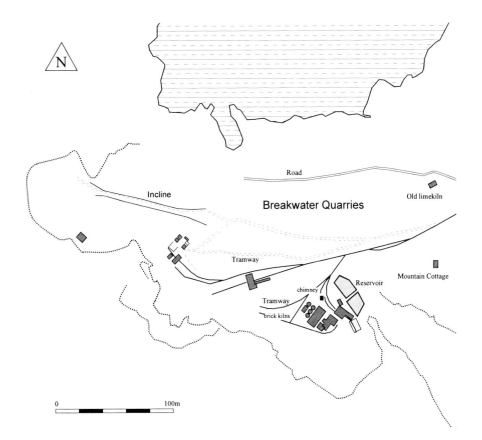

Fig 5
*Holyhead Quarry
in 1900.*

Plate 8 *The completed harbour of refuge in 1873; from* The Illustrated London News.

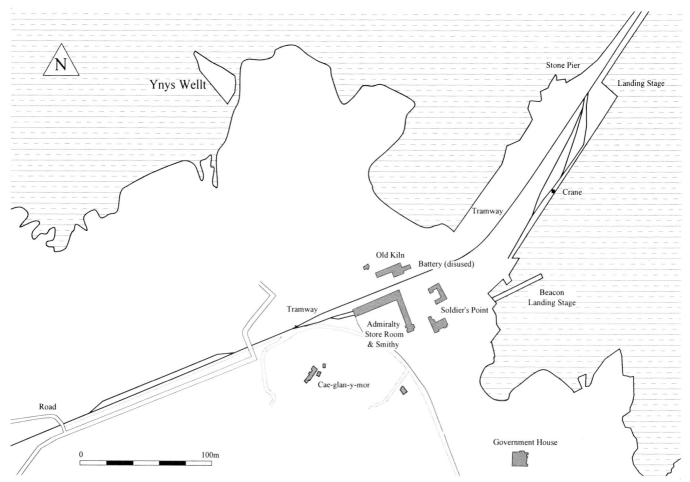

Fig 6 *The breakwater sidings in 1900.*

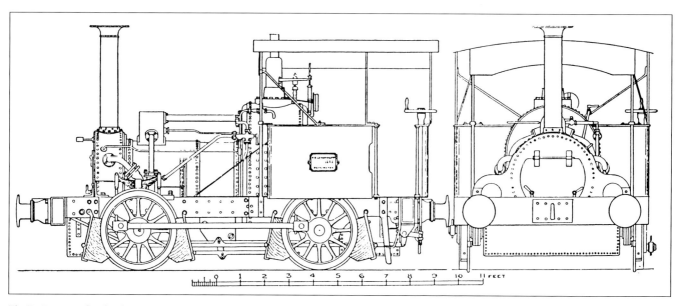

Fig 7 *Front and side elevations of the last 7' gauge locomotive; from Alfred Rosling Bennett's* The Chronicles of Boulton's Siding.

Two more conventional Neilson tank locos were later supplied, of which one (Neilson 697 of 1862) had inside cylinders and the other (Neilson 978 of 1863) had the cylinders outside.

About 250 iron side-tipping wagons were employed of a special "self-righting" design by G. C. Dobson, M.Inst.C.E., the Resident Engineer.

One Longridge engine was named *Prince Albert* as it was employed to take the Prince Consort around the works in 1853 when he inspected them on his way to the Dublin exhibition. *Prince Albert* was again called to the colours in 1873, being employed on similar royal duties when the Prince of Wales (later King Edward VII) came to Holyhead on completion of the works. The Prince and Princess were "conveyed in a train of small wagons, prettily decorated and drawn by a locomotive" to the head of the breakwater where Chichester Fortescue, President of the Board of Trade, read a statement and the Prince declared the breakwater opened.[7]

On completion of the breakwater, *Prince Albert* was retained for maintenance work, but his five sisters were all sold, four of them (*London*, *Holyhead*, *Cambria* and *Queen*) going to the famous dealer, Isaac Watt Boulton of Ashton-under-Lyne, who converted them into stationary engines, whilst the sixth one was sent to Ponta Delgada at São Miguel in the Azores for duties on a breakwater railway there. Amazingly, it is believed to survive at Ponta Delgada to this day. The fate of the Neilson locos is unknown.

The opening of the stone quarry had revealed the existence of silica stone suitable for brick-making, with the result that a few years later the quarry was leased to William Wild and Sons who erected beehive and Scotch kilns, and took over *Prince Albert* and the broad gauge railway. They may possibly have used it for maintenance of the breakwater on behalf of the Board of Trade, but the likelihood is that their own output of bricks left by road.

Plate 9 *The last Holyhead 7' gauge locomotive in steam, 5 March 1912.*   *Courtesy Jim Peden*

---

[7] *Illustrated London News*, vol. 63, 23 August 1873 p. 179 col. c.

Plate 10 *A very derelict* Prince Albert *photographed at an unknown date – presumably between the wars.*   *Courtesy V. J. Bradley*

Plate 11 *A view of the locomotive shed of William Wild and Sons Ltd on 11 May 1958. By then all the 7' gauge track had been removed and the locomotives seen were both conventional standard gauge 0-4-0STs. Andrew Barclay 1584 of 1917 lies out of use on the right, and the working loco, Peckett 1873 of 1934, is seen on the left-hand road.*   *Courtesy E. V. Richards*

By 1910 the Great Breakwater was in need of considerable repair and a contract was awarded to S. Pearson and Son Ltd for this work. They began by laying a new standard gauge line alongside the old broad gauge, employing a Manning Wardle 0-4-0 ST named *Crowhurst* (MW 1384 of 1898) and probably a Hudswell Clark 0-6-0 ST as well. *Crowhurst* had formerly been part of Pearson's large fleet employed on their King George V Dock contract at Hull and on completion of the work in January 1913 was sold to Messrs Wild. For a while it appears that the two railways operated alongside each other, but by 1913, despite a boiler renewal, *Prince Albert* was about worn out, and henceforth only standard gauge was used to maintain the breakwater.[8]

In his classic account of Isaac Watt Boulton's trade in buying up and hiring out elderly steam locomotives, *The Chronicles of Boulton's Siding*, Alfred Rosling Bennett records that during its lengthy career *Prince Albert* was twice proposed for preservation. When reviewing the harbour opening ceremony in its issue of 22 August 1873 the *Engineer* suggested that this "wonderful locomotive" should be displayed on a plinth, and on its withdrawal forty years later Bennett himself attempted to save the locomotive. Although Messrs Wild declined to co-operate, they must have felt some affection for their ancient locomotive. It remained at their works, becoming more and more derelict, until final scrapping in 1945, a very sad loss.

The standard gauge line was relaid with new rail in 1934, at which time a new Peckett 0-4-0ST (Peckett 1873) was purchased. Its boiler was condemned in March 1966 but as coincidentally Messrs Wild and Sons Ltd had just obtained a twelve-month contract for the supply of stone for breakwater repairs, it was necessary for British Railways to provide a replacement diesel locomotive as part of the contract.

The locomotive sent was ED6, one of five John Fowler 0-4-0 150hp diesel mechanical units supplied to B.R. for departmental duties in 1949. However, ED6 gave considerable trouble at Holyhead and was ultimately replaced in June 1967 by two more modern Andrew Barclay locos, nos D2954 and 2955, which remained in service until use of this isolated line ceased in 1979-80.[9] Most of the track was subsequently lifted and the route converted to a road, but a length of 7' gauge rail, bull-head in chairs on stone sleepers, has been preserved on the site of the brickworks, which now forms part of the Holyhead Breakwater Country Park.[10]

---

[8] *Prince Albert* was therefore the last locomotive to work on the 7' gauge in Britain. Three vertical boiler locomotives built for Falmouth Docks by Sara and Burgess in 1860 operated until the mid-1920s, but had been converted to standard gauge *c.* 1892. *Tiny*, the only surviving 7' gauge locomotive in Britain, had been converted to a stationary engine in 1883. See Rowland A. S. Abbott, *op. cit.*, pp. 116–8.

[9] E. V. Richards, *LMS Diesel Locomotives and Railcars* (Railway Correspondence and Travel Society, 1996) pp. 122–7.

[10] Holyhead Breakwater Country Park is open all the year round. Further information can be obtained by 'phoning Mr Edwin Owens, the warden, on 01407 760530.

Lord Newborough and Mr Madocks' "Very Fortunate Circumstance":

a chapter in the development of slate transport in the Vale of Maentwrog

by Gareth Haulfryn Williams

While the main story of the trials and tribulations of the Ffestiniog slate proprietors and William Madocks to improve the transport of slate from quarry to seaport has long been published, new material from the Newborough collection at Caernarfon Record Office has only recently been made available which throws some light on the relationship between the Newborough estate and William Madocks, and on a still-born scheme to export slate through Pwllheli.

The North Wales slate industry in the early nineteenth century attracted countless entrepreneurs, capitalists and quarry operators from across the border: some with names which testified to their wealth or status, such as Rothschild and Palmerston, and others who came to increase their financial and social standing through a closer involvement with the industry – the Turners, Hollands, Cassons and their like. These latter were joined by some local businessmen and minor landowners in the ever-changing alliances and partnerships which brought together enough capital to secure take-notes and crown leases to work the multitude of small quarries which were appearing right round the outlier mountains of the Snowdon massif.

Apart – and perhaps aloof – from this entrepreneurial scramble stood the great landed proprietors of Penrhyn and Faenol; through their own employees the Pennant and Assheton-Smith families controlled and developed the quarries which, over nigh on two centuries, were to develop into the great Penrhyn and Dinorwig operations. These two families controlled a huge share of the industry and, not having to pay royalties or rent to any ground landlord, had the edge when it came to profitability. Blessed with some of the very best slate beds, they controlled the industry and its markets in a way which no incoming investor could hope to do. It was not just the quarrying that these dynasties controlled either; the slate travelled along their private railways to their private ports, often to be transported in their private ships, while their quarrymen lived in cottages and smallholdings on their estates as their tenants.

There was in fact a third family which could, had it wished, have centred its endeavours on the slate industry and perhaps, had it done so, it could have become the greatest slate family of all. The Wynns of Glynllifon in Llandwrog parish some six miles south of Caernarfon had been slowly consolidating and adding to their estates throughout the eighteenth century, largely by prudent marriages to landed heiresses. By the time that Sir Thomas Wynn (elevated to the Irish peerage for political obsequiousness to George III) died in 1807, the Glynllifon family had witnessed the start of slate quarrying on the common lands of their local parishes, as well as on their own land at Glynrhonwy (Llanberis), Cedryn (above Dolgarrog in the Conwy Valley) and on the farms of Cwmbowydd and Maenofferen in Blaenau Ffestiniog.

Sir Thomas Wynn's father, John Wynn, had in fact been granted a crown lease in 1745 to exploit the slate on commons between Llanrug and the Nantlle Valley but neither he nor his son seemingly realised the huge potential. Dr Jean Lindsay details how, in fact, the Wynns lost their minimal rights to other operators on Mynydd Cilgwyn and Cefn Du, Lord Newborough becoming, somewhat improbably, the champion of squatter-quarrymen against the crown agent who from 1794 on was endeavouring to grant leases to a conglomerate of local businessmen.[1] Maybe this was a fit of pique on Lord Newborough's part rather than feeling for the local men since his son tried to throw those selfsame squatters off the Cilgwyn commons a quarter of a century later when he attempted to secure an enclosure act – an attempt to be

---

[1] Jean Lindsay, *A History of the North Wales Slate Industry* (Newton Abbott, 1974) p. 67.

foiled again by the squatters' determination and some brilliant lobbying of Parliament (of which the second Lord was a member), and which deprived Glynllifon of the chance of suitable slate quarrying land near to home.[2]

One of the reasons that the Glynllifon family, despite being proprietor of several very substantial quarries, is often disregarded as a major player in the slate industry, may be this lack of one single large quarry in its back yard so to speak. The Nantlle-Cilgwyn quarry area developed in a fragmented way. Another is that the first Lord died leaving huge debts which took thirty years or so to clear, so that investment was a less attractive option than setting quarries out to entrepreneurial groupings, where someone else's capital would be involved, and a cash income could be expected. The long period between the first Lord's death in 1807, and the coming of age of the second Lord in 1823, when other quarries were surging forward, saw management by a timid and conservative set of absentee trustees who were loath to venture upon any new initiative.[3]

It is, however, clear that such quarrying operations as were being carried out were a mixture of direct involvement and (at least where speculators had secured mineral leases from the first Lord) the taking of royalties on others' endeavours. The records are somewhat patchy, but the trustee's local representative (William Glynne Griffith of Bodegroes, Pwllheli, one of the county's principal lawyers and himself a minor landowner) ensured that this correspondence relating to the estate was filed and preserved, thus starting a tradition perpetuated by the second and third Lords Newborough (who were very much hands-on managers of their own affairs); the bundles of such correspondence for most years from 1818 onwards have been preserved and are only now becoming available as the catalogues are issued by the Caernarfon Record Office.

There is mention in the letters of Glynrhonwy, of Cedryn, of the various negotiations regarding the Ffestiniog quarries, and the complicated liaisons, federations and factions which were, perhaps, inescapable in an area where various proprietors struggled for supremacy in the battle not only to produce slate but to ship it away to the markets on the most economic terms. There is of course a wealth of information on all aspects of estate management, family and public life as well. What follows is little more than a footnote to work published already, but it may serve

to illustrate the virtual quarry which the records are for the historian who chooses to mine them.

*   *   *   *

There is perhaps no need to rehearse here the story of how William Alexander Madocks came to the Traeth Mawr area of south Caernarfonshire, built the Cob across the Afon Glaslyn to reclaim large areas of land and endeavoured to encourage the slate trade to use his harbours, initially at Ynys y Cyngar and (after an 1821 Act of Parliament gave consent) at Ynys y Tywyn, later to be called Porthmadog.[4] It is also well known how a tramway was used for the construction of the Cob and how it remained *in situ*, presumably for maintenance work, after being relaid to repair the serious breach of the embankment in 1812.[5]

Plate 12 *William Alexander Madocks in his old age – a portrait by an unknown artist in Caernarfon archives.*

[2] David Thomas, *Cau'r Tiroèdd Comin* (Lerpwl, d.d.) tt. 58–9.
[3] Evidenced in the Newborough Estate Letters. CRO XD2/15015 ff.
[4] M. J. T. Lewis *How Ffestiniog got its Railway* (Caterham 1968) pp. 8–9, *Sails on the Dwyryd* (Penrhyndeudraeth 1989) pp. 65–77.
[5] J. I. C. Boyd *The Festiniog Railway Vol. 1 – History and Route* (Oakwood Press, 1975) pp. 16–17.

Slate was initially carried down from the various Ffestiniog quarries either in panniers or carts, loaded onto barges near Maentwrog and then transhipped at Ynys Cyngar, until the first (Holland's) quay was opened at the new Porth Madog in 1824. This was but one development which created a greater imperative to improve communications between quarry and sea. One other factor, which is clear from the Newborough letters, is that the coming-of-age of the second Lord, and his arrival back in North Wales after completing education and foreign travel – and indeed his virtual exile from his native area at the insistence of his non-resident guardians and trustees – gave a further (if minor) impetus to the flurry of activity at this time.

It is clear that one at least of the Newborough quarries in Blaenau Ffestiniog – probably Foty or "Chwarel Lord" – was being worked directly by the estate. In August 1823, the resident engineer on the Menai Bridge, W. A. Provis, wrote to Lord Newborough asking whether he might lease slate ground at Ffestiniog, he "having lately had an opportunity of examining the slate rock on your Lordship's estate near Ffestiniog."[6] It is intriguing to wonder why Provis had gone to Ffestiniog in 1823, when the Menai and Conwy bridges and Telford's Holyhead Road must have taken so much of his time; in 1820 he had drawn up a scheme for a road across Traeth Bach for Madocks, and in 1824–5 he surveyed the line of the abortive Ffestiniog and Port Madoc Railway. He certainly found employment from Lord Newborough elsewhere on the estate in 1824,[7] but did his Ffestiniog visit herald an involvement in railway building prior to 1824? At any account, Provis did not find the entry to the Welsh slate industry he sought; a swift reply from W. Glynne Griffith scotched any doubt about his Lordship's intentions: "respecting his slate property in Merionethshire ... his Lordship has determined upon working it himself."[8]

In the light of this determination, it is not surprising that the issue of facilitating the carriage of slate looms large in the estate correspondence. As early as March 1823 there was much to-ing and fro-ing discussing a right of road from his Lordship's Ffestiniog quarries over land belonging to Dr Wynne of Bangor called the Pengwern estate and land belonging to Mr Bankes of Dolymoch. An early solution was desired by Griffith, the estate lawyer, "as the season for active operations in Lord Newborough's Merionethshire

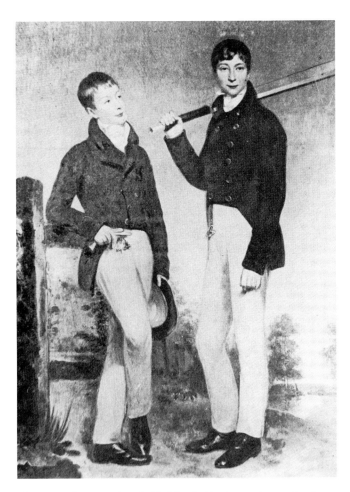

Plate 13 *The second and third Lords Newborough as schoolboys. The second lord stands on the right, the third on the left. By an anonymous artist.*

concerns is at hand" – suggesting that slate conveyance (if not production) was very much a summertime activity.[9]

The term "road" could be open to some doubt, since a railway vocabulary had by then hardly been adopted, and in April 1824 Madocks was discussing with his agent two alternative routes for a railway – basically the later Ffestiniog Railway or one with a heavy gradient at the top end, crossing the Wynne and Bankes lands, and proceeding along the valley floor from Dolymoch.[10] The Newborough estate could hardly have been ignorant of rail's benefits – the Penrhyn line had been running for a quarter of a century,[11] the Dinorwig quarry was shortly to be linked to the port[12] and there had been talk of a railway from

---

6 CRO XD2/15455.
7 CRO XD2A/1646.
8 CRO XD2/15469.
9 CRO XD2/15363.
10 M. J. T. Lewis, *How Ffestiniog got its Railway* p. 11.
11 Jean Lindsay, *op. cit.*, p. 172.
12 J. I. C. Boyd, *Narrow Gauge Railways in North Caernarvonshire Vol. 3* (Headington, 1986) p. 10.

Ffestiniog as early as 1820 when Madocks had already suggested a railroad past Dolymoch.[13] Most tellingly of all, the Faingoch quarry at Cilgwyn in the Newborough's home parish had a railroad of sorts as early as 1810.[14] On the other hand, a lot of road building had been going on in the immediate area of the Ffestiniog quarries, Samuel Holland being one operator to do this in the 1820s,[15] so one cannot be sure that in March 1823 the "right of road" sought was for a railroad.

Such a road was however not immediately forthcoming. Dr Wynne and Mr Bankes, no doubt aware of their stranglehold on the quarries' development, proved difficult, arguing over the sale of a liberty of road versus the taking of tolls or royalties. Terms were only set in June 1824 when John Maughan, on behalf of the Wynne and Bankes interests, promised W. Glynne Griffith that he would meet "later on in the year" to finalise matters.[16] By this time, as we shall see, whatever the initial interpretation placed on the use of the use of the word "road", Lord Newborough

was actively talking in terms of a rail link between quarry and sea, a possibility first mentioned, it would seem, by George Bettiss, Lord Newborough's agent. Writing of a meeting he had with Dr Wynne, Bettiss reported on 13 October 1823 to Griffith, that "I had asked him if he had any objection to consent to our having a road or railway through his property upon being paid such a Compensation as a Jury of his County would award to him, to which he said, he would consider it and consult with Mr Bankes."[17]

The amount of correspondence about this "road", be it railroad or otherwise, shows how crucial it was thought to be for the development of the quarry business, although Bettiss, in the same letter as that previously quoted, suggests cunningly "whether it is not best to let the matter rest for the present and get our Slates down the best way we can till they are shown that we can do without their accommodation".

*   *   *   *

Plate 14 *The Vale of Maentwrog near Dolymoch, the area owned by Dr Wynne, 1823.*

---

[13] M. J. T. Lewis, *op. cit.*, p. 9.
[14] Jean Lindsay, *op. cit.*, p. 75.
[15] Jean Lindsay, *op. cit.*, p. 170.
[16] CRO XD2/15916.
[17] CRO XD2/15557.

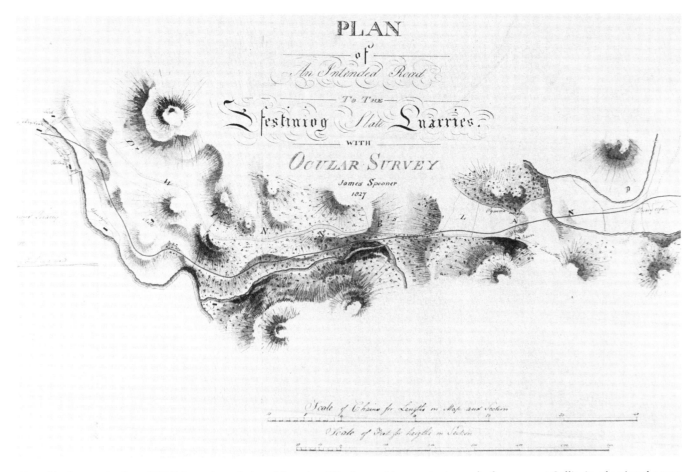

PLAN
of
An Intended Road
TO THE
Ffestiniog Slate Quarries.
WITH
OCULAR SURVEY

James Spooner
1827

Plate 15 *Spooner's plan of 1827 for an intended road from Lord Newborough's quarries towards the quays at Gelligrin, showing the area controlled by Dr Wynne which was the subject of dispute earlier in the decade.*

Wynne and Bankes were, however, not the only cause of frustration for the Newborough quarrying interests. It appears from a letter addressed by W. Glynne Griffith from Hay, Breckonshire, to William Madocks in November 1823 that the latter was also occasioning the estate some concern. Hay, incidentally, is close to the Tregunter home of William Madocks' wife (whom he had married in 1818), but we should not perhaps read too much into such a location for Griffith's visit, as Lord Newborough and his brother, Spencer Bulkeley, had connections there through their former tutor's family of Wilkins or de Winton as they became. Perhaps more significantly, Hay was the terminus of the Brecon to Hay Railway which Griffith could hardly fail to notice.[18]

Griffith and Bettiss had debated whether or not they should discuss various undisclosed matters with Madocks the previous month, Griffith (the senior of the two estate servants) decreeing it unwise to do so. Madocks was obviously wanting to bargain with the Newborough faction, possibly to secure their support for his schemes.[19] By November, however, while avoiding a personal meeting, Griffith could not avoid sending a response of sorts to Madocks, which is worth quoting in full:

Hay, Breconshire
13 Nov 1823

My Dear Sir,
I felt myself obliged to delay answering your kind communication until I had an opportunity of making Ld. Newborough thoroughly acquainted with the purport of it. His Lordship has desired me to express to you how sensibly he feels your kind disposition to afford him all the facilities & conveniences in your power to bring your slate property down for exportation & the interest her entertains in

---

[18] Elizabeth Beazley, *Madocks and the Wonder of Wales* (London, 1967) pp. 204–6.
[19] CRO XD2/15597, 15601.

furthering any measure which can conduce to the improvement and benefit of that portion of the County of Carnarvon in which you are more immediately interested – it has always occurred to me that nothing could be more desirable than that Lord Newborough should avail himself of the advantages and accommodation which Port Madoc in a state of perfection would afford him, but having observed a lapse of two years since the passing of the last act for the improvement of that port without anything like and effort made to arrange it may cause, I fear, the necessity of directing my attention to some other Quarter where those advantages & accommodations might be secured, & with this view I recommend to Lord N. To purchase the Ginlet Rock at the mouth of the Port of Pwllheli & some land contiguous, where I was satisfied that at a small expense an import & export Trade might be carried on upon an extensive scale. Tho' I took this step I was at the same time unwilling to abandon all hopes of something turning out favourable to Port Madoc, & I assure you the rect. of your letter & its general tenor afforded me the most lively satisfaction, arising out of the impression it made upon me that your wanted energy had been awakened to the importance of bringing it to that state of perfection which it appears to be so desirable it shd. arrive at.

Sensibly determined upon working his own Quarry, & the magnitude of his Ldship's prospects from that source appear to be incalculable. There are not doubt many weighty consideration connected with this concern, & knowing how capable you are of offering suggestions worthy of adoption, I beg that you will not hesitate in entering upon an exposition of your views to any length you may think necessary & they shall receive the earliest attention Mrs Griffith & myself feel infinitely obliged by your kind invitation. Believe me My dear Sir,

Yours very truly
WGG[20]

This letter, despite its very civil tone, is in fact quite critical of the delays which had beset the development of Porthmadog. The fact that the Newborough trustees had insisted on free passage of slates across the Cob tramway in Madock's 1821 harbour bill, as the price for their withdrawing their petition against the bill,[21] indicates their

enthusiasm for facilities to be developed at the New Porthmadog; and now, two years later, little had happened. The Gimlet Rock scheme may appear to be a strange affair at first sight, since Pwllheli is some twelve miles west of Traeth Mawr, and taking the slate there would have doubled the distance to a trans-shipping point; on the other hand, Ynys Cyngar was an unsatisfactory harbour and once the slates had been put on board the river vessels at Maentwrog, if they could make Ynys Cyngar presumably in clement weather they could go as far as Pwllheli. If that was the best site for a reasonable harbour (and it was nearer the safe sealanes) then it might have been a price worth paying.

The suggestion was certainly not just put in the letter to frighten Madocks into action. For Griffith had already expressed his misgivings as to Madocks' ability to develop Porthmadog, and nor were those limited to himself. On 29 July 1823 John Ellis, a Pwllheli solicitor acting for the vendors of one John Humphreys' estate, which included the Gimlet Rock (an outcrop of granite worked as a stone quarry at the mouth of Pwllheli harbour) had written to Griffith asking whether Lord Newborough "would find it convenient" to purchase the whole estate. "Mr Holland" (undoubtedly Samuel Holland the Ffestiniog quarry proprietor) had asked the price of the Gimlet. "No doubt" Ellis continued, "Mr Holland wants the Gimlet to Erect a Quay to Deposit his slates."[22] Griffith saw the potential as had Holland, but George Bettiss, the Newborough agent who was more intimately concerned with the Ffestiniog quarries, was doubtful, and rushed (on 31 July) to put his point: "about the Gimlet point ... it has always been a hobby with me to secure that point as I have always considered it a Key to the Town and Trade of Pwllheli and if ever you have the most distant intention of establishing that as a Bathing place be sure to secure that property. I do not agree with Mr Holland or yourself in the plan of establishing it as a port for the Shipping of the Ffestiniog Slates."[23]

In the event, Madocks took the hint and stirred himself to press on with work on the quays so that, at least by September 1824, ships of up to 60 tonnes' burden could tie up at the new quay,[24] and the Gimlet, although bought for the Newborough estate, never became a competitor for Porthmadog. He had, however, been seriously worried. By May 1824, Lord Newborough was openly interested in seeing a railway built to carry the slate; in this at least he

[20] CRO XD2/15607.
[21] M. J. T. Lewis, *op. cit.*, pp. 10–11.
[22] CRO XD2/15414.
[23] CRO XD2/15417.
[24] Elizabeth Beazley, *op. cit.*, p. 217.

was in tune with Madocks who had commissioned a survey of possible routes on 22 April.[25] George Bettiss wrote from London on 15 May to describe a meeting he had with Madocks:

> Mr Madocks was confined of the Gout when I arrived in town with the Draft and I did not get any thing forward till Thursday when I presented him with the Draft Deed to Lord Newborough of the liberty for his Lordship's laying his railway over Mr M.'s property whenever he may have occasion, to which he did not object, but proposed the insertion of a protecting clause to guard against Lord Newborough's using such railway to carry his slates to any other place than Port Madock, he dwelled much on the proposed grand stroke of business ...

Madocks went on to suggest to Bettiss that the railway should be effected "by shares", thus getting all the quarry proprietors behind the scheme. Bettiss had to remind Madocks that Lord Newborough had agreed to support the 1821 Harbour Act in return for personal concessions in the waiving of tolls. Madocks then asked for £1200 from Lord Newborough since, although he could get it elsewhere, "he wishes to put the Harbour entirely into his Lordship's hands."[26] The draft deed is extant in the Newborough collection, permitting the railway from his Lordship's quarries to pass over Madocks' land to Porthmadog harbour, while a corresponding agreement made provision for the repair of the railroad across Traeth Mawr by Lord Newborough. This latter deed interestingly confirms the continued existence of the rails across the Cob.[27]

Madocks obviously felt that Newborough was an ideal partner for his endeavours; he was young, wealthy, influential and operating a quarry with problems of getting slate down to the ships – a report by Samuel Smith in January 1824 had described the route from Newborough's quarry as "exceedingly circuitous, very hilly and in a wretched state."[28] Equally the Newborough party felt that a certain distance was best kept between them, since they potentially had the better hand. Madocks, however, the new harbour now open, saw that he needed to continue the dialogue and a final round of correspondence between the parties is preserved, from the autumn of 1824.

In a long and rather repetitive letter penned at the posting-inn of Cernioge near Pentrefoelas on 21 September 1824, Madocks looks forward to a meeting with Lord Newborough and Griffith. He had been visited by "an experienced person from South Wales, taking the levels with exactness through the Vale of Ffestiniog, my object being to demonstrate the *practicability* & *expediency* of a Tram Road up the Vale, not more for the interest of the Mine Proprietors, than the Land-owners, taking for proof & example, the various Tram Roads in the many Vales in Glamorganshire similarly situated, and which have conferred the greatest benefits on the agricultural as well as the mining interests. The back Carriage of Lime & other requisites for improvement, together with the Industry it excites, renders a Tram Road a great blessing to the district ..." Moreover, an engineer, again from South Wales, had satisfied him as to the "favourable nature of the line of the Country." He feared the "unconquerable dulness & obstinacy" of some local landowners, which he saw as a major hurdle to be overcome. Newborough is again being addressed here not so much as a quarryowner as one of the local landed proprietors, and one who had influence over his colleagues. As a manifesto for Madocks' continued enthusiasm for developing the area it is a significant document.[29]

The meeting Madocks hoped to have was apparently for "communicating to you a very important matter for Lord Newborough's consideration which the limits of a letter will not enable me to explain", as he put it in another September letter, to W. Glynne Griffith. This letter includes the intriguing aside that, when they meet, Madocks will be able "to return silver you were so kind as to produce to my signal relief from a distressing embarrassment in the Grand Jury Box."[30] Such a remark cautions us against assuming that all contact between the two sides in the discussion was limited to that recorded in the correspondence.

A social occasion, when Mr and Mrs Griffith at Bodegroes had entertained the Madocks family, had taken place by 3 October 1824, when Madocks sent "Mr Overton's preliminary observations respecting the Tram Road." Relations, on at least a personal level, were extremely cordial, and Madocks took the opportunity to emphasise once more his desire "to promote every wish of his Lordship in this Country ... (as) benefactor to a large district, capable of so much Improvement",[31] a comment all the more remarkable in its obsequiousness coming as it did from an M.P., a substantial landowner and a man more than twice Lord Newborough's age to boot.

However he claimed to "promote every wish" of Lord Newborough, it was not long before tensions arose with

[25] M. J. T. Lewis, *op. cit.*, p. 11.
[26] CRO XD2/15864.
[27] CRO XD2/13296–7.
[28] CRO XD2/15699.
[29] CRO XD2/15989.
[30] CRO XD2/16000.
[31] CRO XD2/16004.

George Bettiss who wrote to Griffith after the Quarter Sessions, where Madocks had sought an order to instigate the harbour dues at Porthmadog. Bettiss was annoyed that Madocks "did not intimate to me his intentions of so doing, so as to give me the opportunity of satisfying myself that the Quay was in such a state as to justify such steps." Bettiss went to Porthmadog where he found "a good deal done and that very well done, but certainly not enough done to justify the order being made", but felt that an appeal against the magistrates who had made the order was of little use since by the next Quarter Sessions, the quay would be in order. Bettiss and Madocks however had heated discussion and Bettiss "told him that I had to blame him for not fulfilling his promise of not giving Lord Newborough a written consent to pass through his land."[32] The question must be posed whether Madocks was trying to avoid the issue, or whether other matters had seemed more pressing. Such inattention to a key player was, however, careless, at a sensitive time shortly before rival bills for a railway were being placed before Parliament, Lord Newborough being apparently one of Madocks' main co-petitioners.[33] Madocks lent the railway plans to Griffith at some time after this *faux-pas* and asked for their return in a letter received on 14 November. He suggested showing him certain aspects of the plan on the ground, as he was anxious to explain them and made sure they were in accord with his Lordship's desires.[34]

One final letter from Madocks is among the Newborough papers, written on 30 November 1824 and posted from Aberystwyth the following day. The letter was addressed to Lord Newborough at Glynllifon but was written to Griffith. Madocks had been detained in Aberystwyth by a bout of illness such as he often had, and was on his way to Tregunter. In it he discussed the forthcoming bill; the plans had been deposited that very day with the Clerk of the Peace at Dolgellau by Mr Bourne, "Mr Overton's man."[35] Mr Oakeley of Tanybwlch was apparently undecided whether or not he should support the scheme and others were hostile to the scheme; Dr Wynne and Mr Bankes are singled out as two persons Madocks would attack "effectively." The purpose of the letter was basically to explain his plan of action to Lord Newborough and solicit his Lordship's views on the printed plan. The shareholding of the railway company was also discussed, with Turner and Co. Being allocated fifty of the 300 shares, Holland and Madocks both taking fifty, and 100 being offered to his Lordship.

This attempt to get a railway authorised and built was eventually to founder,[36] and the collection contains no further letters from Madocks (although reference is made to one full of important matters for discussion which Lord Newborough received on 26 January 1825).[37] The last extant letter already referred to, however, serves almost as a valediction and a declaration of Madocks' assessment of his life's work:

I (need not) point out that the very fortunate circumstances to the Slate Proprietors of the whole labours of my life having prepared them for so excellent a shipping place, when in the old state of the navigation, they could never have carried on an extensive trade, but to the great loss & inconvenience, nor need I point out the Embankment, as having been made, as it were, expressly for the purpose of Laying a Rail Road to the Shipping Place, otherwise unattainable ...[38]

It is surprising that after the failure of the 1825 railroad scheme in Parliament, there is no further discussion for some time of ways of effecting the railway scheme. It would be eleven years before slates started to arrive by rail at Madocks' "shipping place", and by that time Madocks and the second Lord Newborough would both be dead.

* * * *

One curious, almost serendipitous, reference to Madocks remains in the records. The Madocks family had embarked on a long continental holiday in May 1826 and in Paris, on his way home, Madocks was to die on 15 September 1828. A few weeks later, a letter written in French by one F. Olivieri of Florence, was received by Lord Newborough. He offered for sale a suit of armour, formerly in the possession of the Medicis, and purchased by him on behalf of William Madocks, deceased, for the sum of £100.[39] It is not recorded whether or not the Newborough family purchased the armour, but they had a more fitting – and immensely more profitable – legacy from the man who had so obsequiously solicited their support; the "shipping place" and the "Embankment ... expressly for the purpose of laying a Rail Road", which allowed their quarrying interests to flourish beyond their greatest expectations.

[32] CRO XD2/16030.
[33] M. J. T. Lewis, *op. cit.*, pp. 12–14.
[34] CRO XD2/16072.
[35] Overton was the Engineer, Bourne the Surveyor; see J. I. C. Boyd *Festiniog Railway Vol 1 History and Route*, p. 20.
[36] Elizabeth Beazley, *op. cit.*, pp. 217–222.
[37] CRO XD2/16134.
[38] CRO XD2/16083.
[39] CRO XD2/16847.

Quarrymen and Insanity in North Wales:

from the Denbigh Asylum Records

by Dr Pam Michael

Dr Pam Michael considers a number of case studies of men and women from the slate quarry communities of North-west Wales who were committed to the Denbigh Lunatic Asylum, and analyses the social, medical and economic pressures under which they worked.

In 1888 a forty-four year old quarryman and father of three, D.W. from Glandwr, Blaenau Ffestiniog, was admitted to the North Wales Lunatic Asylum. Six months prior to his committal he had met with an accident to his foot whilst working at the Quarry. He was treated for his injury at the Oakley Hospital, and over a period of five months made a good recovery. However, soon after discharge his mind became affected. According to the asylum case notes, he appears to have "been labouring under the idea that his long residence in hospital would incapacitate him from further employment".[1] "About a month ago", the doctor's summary of the case continues, "he became low and desponding and on going to his work would not take care of himself viz. the blasting and so on of the rocks. Has latterly become worse, refusing to take his food and restless and sleepless day and night." D.W. was described as a steady, temperate and industrious man, and no doubt the experience of being discharged from hospital, almost immediately to resume his responsibilities as breadwinner and return to the quarries, must have proved unsettling, if not traumatic. The medical certificate signed by the local doctor stated that D.W. "Labours under delusions that he will get no work anymore in the quarries, and that he must leave the place. He also sees the managers in different places in the House. He is constantly untying his boot laces – even at it for hours at a time." A neighbour further certified, before a magistrate, that D.W. had "on more than one occasion taken a knife in his hand and threatened his own wife". This quarryman was finally discharged in 1913, having been a patient at the asylum for twenty-five years.

The description of this man's illness, and the conjunction of his physical injury and subsequent "mental instability", his anxieties about his ability to carry out his work, his carelessness in the face of occupational dangers, the intrusion of his fears concerning his job into the privacy of his home, and finally his turning violently toward his wife – these "symptoms" of illness, derived from his medical case notes, show how intimately bound up with the concerns of everyday life are the clinical and medical conditions of the insane. Madness presents as primarily a social illness,[2] so much so that some writers have even gone so far as to assert that there is no such thing as mental illness – only "problems of everyday living".[3]

The case-records of the North Wales Lunatic Asylum at Denbigh (plate 16), opened in 1848, provide a window on the everyday concerns, anxieties, and behaviour of a broad spectrum of working people from the mid-nineteenth century through to recent times. Partly a subscription hospital, (with contributions towards its building from local gentry, quarry owners, and quarry workers) but primarily a public asylum financed and supported by the five counties of North Wales, Anglesey, Carnarvonshire, Flintshire, Denbighshire and Merionethshire, it served the whole of North Wales, until its closure in 1995.

The run-down of the hospital posed the question of what would become of this rich medical and historical resource. A number of substantial deposits of material had been transferred to the local archive, but a considerable range of material remained in the hospital. In 1993 the School of History and Welsh History of the University of

---

[1] Denbighshire Record Office, Ruthun, HD/1/365 Case no. 4004, date of admission 13 September 1888.
[2] Roy Porter, *A Social History of Madness* (George Weidenfeld and Nicolson Ltd., London, 1987).
[3] Thomas Szasz, *The Myth of Mental Illness; Foundations of a Theory of Personal Conduct* (Dell, New York, 1961).

Plate 16 *The North Wales Lunatic Asylum, Denbigh.*

Wales Bangor, received a grant from the Wellcome Trust to support an in-depth study of the papers, and to research the history of mental illness and society in North Wales. This article is based on a small section of that research, but serves to illustrate the case for having the material both preserved and analysed.

Many writers have emphasised the arduous physical conditions faced by the quarrymen, their exposure to extremes of cold and wet, the effects on their health, the frequency with which they experienced rheumatism and arthritis, the high risk from accidents, and the common incidence of chest complaints, and tuberculosis.[4] Quarriers, rockmen and miners had an average expected age of only 48 years.[5] R. Merfyn Jones writes of the quarryman carrying, during his life "... the involuntary badges of his identity, in particular, his ill-health".[6]

Whilst there is nothing to suggest that quarrymen were more prone to suffer from mental illness than any other group of workers in North Wales in the nineteenth century, nonetheless, when their case histories are analysed in detail, they do constitute a distinct group amongst the patients at the Asylum. The details of their committal, and the background information noted down by the medical officer at the Asylum, provide a rare insight into what otherwise has remained a hidden side of the work, and personal and community life of the quarrymen.

The Wellcome Trust-funded research project, with support from Clwyd Health Authority, took a 10% sample of all patients admitted to the hospital from its opening in 1848, through to the outbreak of the Second World War. During the period 1875 to 1914 around 10–12% of the males in this sample were quarrymen. They are probably not over-represented as a group, since this proportion

---

[4] Jean Lindsay, *A History of the North Wales Slate Industry* (David and Charles, Newton Abbott, 1974) pp.234–242; Emyr Jones, *Canrif y Chwarelwyr* (Gwasg Gee, Denbigh, 1964), *Bargen Dinorwig* (Ty ar y Graig, Caernarfon, 1980); R. Merfyn Jones, *The North Wales Quarrymen, 1874–1922* (University of Wales Press, Cardiff, 1981).

[5] R. Merfyn Jones, *op.cit.* p.35.

[6] *Ibid.*, p. 34.

seems to do no more than reflect their importance in the labour force of North Wales.[7] A number of government enquiries were carried out which reported not only on the working conditions in the quarries,[8] but also on the physical health of the quarrymen, and the Denbigh records augment these other sources in valuable ways.

Few people have written openly, or at length, about mental illness in Wales. The novel of Caradog Prichard, *Un Nos Ola Leuad* ("Full Moon"),[9] is quite exceptional in dealing directly with the experience of insanity. Having worked closely with the asylum records for some years now, I still regard this novel as a very honest portrayal of the intensely personal torment of witnessing a mental breakdown, beautifully evoked through the eyes of a child growing up in a quarrying community. It offers a sensitive literary insight into the harsh experiences which often accompanied a woman's slide into insanity.

Apart from the legal aspects of committal, there were many reasons why people feared mental illness and were shamed and stigmatised by it, in a way that was not evident with any other form of illness. Individuals attracted attention when they began to behave in ways that were socially unacceptable. Committal was often precipitated by scenes of violence, destruction of clothes and property, offensive use of language, extreme and often embarrassing acts, such as outbursts of preaching in public, singing, shouting, and running naked into the street. People were diagnosed mad by their families and neighbours, because of their inappropriate and anti-social behaviour. Usually it was only then that a doctor was summoned. Some patients were admitted having first been in the workhouse, a very few came from prison, and some were apprehended by the police, either wandering insane, or for attempting suicide, or for outrageous behaviour in a public place. Therefore it was this precipitating behaviour that marked the person as insane, and which led to their committal to the asylum. They had come into conflict with the expected norms of behaviour of their society. It is this that makes the study of mental illness so different from the history of any other form of illness. We learn not only about the form of disease, but also about the social norms which were transgressed;

the case papers itemise the personal, family and social conflicts, and the life events which led up to and culminated in the patient's compulsory committal to the asylum.[10]

Mental illness was little understood. We still do not fully understand it today. It was feared and dreaded because recovery was unpredictable, and because for many people life would never be the same again. It is interesting that in a lecture given by Dr R. Alun Roberts in Penygroes in 1968, based on recollections of his own experiences of being brought up in the area, he chose to refer to the alarm caused by mental illness, and the help and support required by members of the insane person's family:

> Mental illness was also a cause of terror and anguish, and a regular call to neighbours to help soothe the effects of the disturbing attacks that perplexed families in their turn – even now a spectre which haunts the area.[11]

The records of the North Wales Hospital illustrate graphically the significance of these comments. R.Alun Roberts was one of Wales' foremost authorities on agriculture, and his intimate knowledge of the small-holding and quarrying communities of North Wales made him a fascinating and popular speaker. He had a sure grasp of the issues which affected people's everyday lives.

There is of course a perennial problem in researching medical history in that many causes of illness were not recognised at the time, whereas many things that we might now regard as incidental were seen as central then. Some nineteenth century doctors viewed the workings of the body as intimately connected with the health of the mind, and thus regarded constipation, for instance, as a serious disorder directly threatening the sanity of the sufferer. This diagnosis might entail for the patient a course of purgative treatment that we might consider draconian. Therefore in terms of contemporary opinion it would be significant that all of the doctors giving evidence to the Committee of Inquiry into the Conditions in the Open Quarries held in 1893, drew particular attention to the quarrymen's habit of drinking nothing all day but stewed tea, arguing meanwhile that the high amounts of tannin resulted in a

---

[7] There are two serious problems in analysing the statistics. Firstly, the decennial Census of Occupations records the numbers working in "mines and quarries". There are far fewer miners than there are quarrymen admitted to the hospital, so whether the one is over-represented at the expense of the other is difficult to ascertain. Quarrying predominated in the western counties of North Wales, mining in the east. It may be that the relieving officers, the key persons responsible for arranging a legal "certificate of lunacy" which would dispatch the patient to the asylum, were more active and responsive to problems identified as insanity amongst the quarrymen of Carnarvonshire, than their counterparts amongst the miners of Flintshire. Hence a difference in referrals would not necessarily imply a difference in incidence. Secondly, the asylum did not follow the same rules of recording occupations as the census enumerators. They relied on self-reportage, or on the word of family or relieving officer. Therefore if a man referred to himself as a "labourer" then he was recorded as such on the admissions papers to the hospital, even though he may have been a labourer in the quarries.

[8] *Report of the Quarry Committee of Inquiry, 1893; Report of the Departmental Committee upon Merionethshire Slate Mines, 1895.*

[9] Caradog Prichard, *Un Nos Ola Leuad* (Gwasg Gwalia, Caernarfon, 1988).

[10] Voluntary admissions did not occur until after the passing of the 1930 Mental Treatment Act.

[11] Robert Alun Roberts, *Y tyddynnwr chwarelwr yn Nyffryn Nantlle: atgofion am Ddyffryn Nantlle*, (Caernarfon: Llyfrgell Sir Caernarfon, 1969 – Darlith Flynyddol Llyfrgell Penygroes, 1968).

leathery lining to the stomach and severe digestive problems. Dyspepsia, asserted Dr Evan Roberts of Penygroes, was the chief cause of disease amongst the quarrymen. During the day the men had little to eat, and only a little bread and butter before they left home in the morning.[12] John William, surgeon to the Penrhyn Quarry Hospital, argued that : "If they could provide themselves with better food in the quarry it would be better for them. The worst of it is that they take a heavy meal at night, and go to bed soon afterwards. They are subject to palsy on that account, and also congestion of the brain."[13] In terms of today's terminology, the doctors were attributing the quarrymen's ill-health to the life-style which they had chosen to adopt. Dr R. H. Mills Roberts, who was surgeon to the Dinorwic quarries and hospital, went so far as to argue that the occupation as such was "very healthy".[14]

Displayed in the medical testimony given to this Parliamentary Committee was a tendency to blame the quarrymen themselves, and also to some extent their wives, who were seen as largely responsible for the failure to provide an adequate diet. This is also true in regard to the evidence on accidents, which were portrayed as being mainly due to the negligence of the workmen, their carelessness and disregard for safety procedures. The local doctors in the quarrying areas invariably seen to have adopted this "personalistic" form of explanation for the quarrymen's ills.

A close reading of the case notes of the quarrymen sent to the asylum does reveal the extent of physical injuries endured by them, and give some indications of the psychological reactions which they might suffer. D.W. was not the only quarryman whose physical injury had precipitated an attack of "insanity". Another quarryman from Blaenau Ffestiniog, D.L., was admitted to the North Wales Lunatic Asylum in August 1897.[15] On his committal certificate it stated that "he does not sleep and will not go to work. He talks incoherently and at times gets violent." But the asylum doctor added the following observations: "Patient fractured his leg on the 24th December, 1896 (it was a compound fracture of the tibia). Soon afterwards a change was noticed in him and the injury is undoubtedly the cause of his mental disorder. The symptoms are now those of ordinary melancholia. He is reported to have been a steady and hard working man." For a person such as this the loss of mobility and of confidence associated with an

injury of this type, must have made an early return to work such as quarrying, which required a high degree of physical stamina, really very daunting. Slate quarrymen began their day by descending ladders to the level of the rock faces, and ended it with climbing back up again. Throughout the day the men would work on ledges, where a stumble or a loss of balance could lead to death, and where blasting and falls of rock represented continuous danger. Yet clearly there was an assumption that as soon as a wound had healed the male breadwinner should resume his duties, and any reluctance to do so was viewed as shirking. The absence of any insurance, industrial compensation, or welfare state system to support the families of these victims, must have added enormously to the feelings of overwhelming responsibility. This might be expected to have a demoralising and depressive effect on men, even when healthy, and more so after suffering an accident.

D.L. was described as a man of below average height, fair development and moderately well nourished, but "low and depressed with no energy". In the North Wales Asylum he became deluded, imagining that his wife and family were there, and hearing voices. By the following year he was reported to be in good health, eating and sleeping well and working on the hospital farm, although he was "very reticent". He was not discharged until 1900, aged 51, three years after his admittance.

Amongst the cases treated at the North Wales Asylum were a number of quarrymen and quarry labourers who suffered from epilepsy. This must have been hazardous not only for the man but for his fellow workers. Dr John William told, in his evidence to the 1893 Committee of Inquiry, how he had one patient, who was subject to fits, who was in the habit of being sent into the Penrhyn Quarry Hospital "nearly every other day". It is indicative, surely, of the level of necessity that must have forced men such as this to take work in so dangerous an occupation.

Some epileptic sufferers became very violent around the period of the onset of fits. A quarryman who was admitted to the asylum in 1875 had threatened to murder his mother, and the lodgers gave testimony that he was threatening to strike them without provocation.[16] In the asylum he proved to be very quarrelsome and violent; he got into a fight with another epileptic patient whom he kicked violently in the abdomen and who died the following

12 *Report of the Quarry Committee of Inquiry, 1893*, evidence of Dr Evan Roberts, par. 73–82.
13 *Ibid.*, evidence of Dr J. William, 267.
14 *Ibid.*, evidence of Dr Mills Roberts. Interestingly, Dr Mills Roberts was to establish his medical career on the basis of publications relating to cases of head injuries treated by him at the quarry hospital. See "Dinorwic Quarry Hospital: cases of head injury" *British Medical Journal* 15 August 1903, also for treatment of other accidents reported by him in *Transactions of the Clinical Society of London* vol. 30.
15 Denbigh Record Office HD/1/370, Case no. 5271, date of admission 23 August 1897.
16 Denbigh Record Office HD/1/360, Case no. 2427, date of admission 20 February 1875.

day from a rupture of the ileum. After a succession of epileptic attacks, this quarryman died in the asylum in 1878. Epilepsy was at this time still widely regarded as a form of mental illness.

Head injuries were particularly dangerous, and could seriously incapacitate the victim. It is really quite extraordinary how some of these men managed to continue working in an industry which required so much physical stamina. R.J.R. was a 34 year old slate quarryman living at Gwastadnant, Llanberis, when he was committed to the asylum in 1891.[17] He had worked regularly at the quarry until about a fortnight before his committal, when he had become insane. It was his third attack of insanity, though this was the first time he had been sent to the asylum. He is described for us by the hospital doctors:

Patient is a very tall man 6ft. 2ins. height and although thin is not badly built. Face pleasant but expression marred by a large scar and depression over right eye. The whole frontal eminence being as it were driven in and the site of a severe depressed fracture can be readily made out. The right eyeball more prominent that the left, and there is also considerable strabismus of same eye. He states that it was fractured at age of 14 and that he had another severe injury in same spot at 26. Shortly after injury he began to have fits but several members of his family are also epileptic. Fits average one a month but have lately become more numerous.

R.J.R. suffered a fit shortly after his admittance to hospital and became violent and unmanageable and so was confined to a locked room. The doctor stated that the patient, when free from epileptic attack, was "an intelligent and well disposed man ... Very anxious to return home and is evidently very fond of his family." The doctor was very anxious to see if somehow the epilepsy could be kept under control. The hospital had by now begun experimenting with bismuth as a treatment for epilepsy. The patient was discharged a couple of months after with advice from the doctor on how to cope with the attacks, and a prescription for medicine to take whenever the fits became more numerous.

The dangerousness of the occupation was common to all who worked there, and whilst many men were injured, some were killed. The Quarry Committee of Enquiry showed that in the ten-year period from 1883 to 1892, there had been 110 fatal accidents in the slate quarries of Caernarvonshire. However, they remarked on the difficulty

of obtaining firm statistics, and made recommendations regarding the details to be recorded in coroners' statistics.[18] The surgeon to the Oakley Hospital, for instance, reported that during the year to October 1870 he had attended to 1,072 casualties.[19] Open any of the bound volumes of newspapers from the late nineteenth century housed in the University of Wales, Bangor and you will come across references to quarrying accidents. The quarry owners and managers combed the pages of the newspapers and sought to refute any reports which they regarded as unfavourable to the quarry owners. On 2 August 1893, Mr Prichard, the Working Manager of the Penrhyn Quarry, wrote to the *Manchester Guardian* to complain about a report published in their newspaper about an accident which had taken place at the Penrhyn quarry in which a crane had tipped over killing a workman. According to the original report a "large piece of slate rock fell from an upper gallery and threw the crane over." Not so, according to Mr Prichard, who stated that "instead of a large piece of rock falling from an upper gallery, a comparatively small piece came down from a height not exceeding five feet above the floor of the gallery on which the men were working. The movement of the piece of rock was observed by the men who stood close by watching it come down; contrary to their expectation, the stone knocked over the crane, which in falling caught deceased as he was running off." Thus the manager and the owner sought to lay the blame squarely with the workmen.

Lord Penrhyn personally visited the scene of the accident, and he found that the fatality was solely due to the carelessness of the men composing the party, of whom one fell a victim to their own indifference to risk, and felt it his duty to inflict some punishment upon the men who were at work with the deceased in order to impress upon them, and the workmen generally, the responsibility which rests with them of taking proper precautions for their own safety and that of their fellow workmen; and it is to be hoped that the suspension of the bargain takers in question, until after the end of the next quarry month, will have the desired effect.[20]

Such punitive language and action displayed little in the way of sympathy for the victim. There must have been an ever-present level of tension among the workmen. Many of the quarrymen who gave evidence to the Quarry Committee of Enquiry emphasised the danger of falling rocks, and stated that a simple way to reduce the hazard would be to

[17] Denbigh Record Office HD/1/365, Case no. 4262, date of admission 15 January 1891.
[18] *Report by the Quarry Committee of Inquiry* (London; H.M.S.O., December 1893) appendix II, pp. 4–5 and evidence of Dr William Ogle, pp. 77–84.
[19] Jean Lindsay, *op. cit.*, p. 238.
[20] *North Wales Chronicle*, 12 August 1893, p. 7, col.g.

employ men to clear the stone from the edge of the galleries periodically, and to have qualified men to inspect the workplace for safety. The system of letting divisions of the rock face to a gang of skilled quarrymen for a bargain, was conducive only to exacting the greatest possible output from the quarries, and not to ensuring safety standards. To make their bargain the men could not afford to spend time in the unproductive task of clearing waste rock, and it was said that the galleries were often strewn with debris. No doubt, as the Revd John Rowlands observed of Welsh workers generally in 1869, the dread of illness and its consequences for families served to heighten their sense of exploitation.[21]

Faced with enormously powerful employers, the quarrymen themselves could only hope to influence their conditions of work through a strong combination. Thus from the very beginnings of their unionism they had sought to enforce unity in order to gain strength. This was inevitably at the expense of any of those who did not conform, and the methods and tenacity with which not only the quarrmen but also the community in which they lived enforced sanction against them is legendary. They were labelled *cynffonwyr, bradwyr*, ("toadies", "traitors"), they were spat upon, refused lodging, they could not enter certain shops or pubs, and when the strikers returned to work they refused to work alongside the men who had betrayed them; there were even rumours of threatened accidents befalling the "blacklegs". Much of this information has been carried in popular oral tradition, but occasionally incidents such as one in August, 1893, were reported in the newspapers. After a strike at the Llechwedd quarry, some of the men, notably those most involved in organising the strike, had not been taken back. A disturbance had broken out, and according to the report:

> ... It appeared that a number of men attacked an old man named Hughes in an upper mill and dragged him out, attempting, it is alleged, to throw him over a precipice. Had they succeeded the man would have met with instant death, but fortunately the man slipped out of their grasp and ran for safety into the quarry office. The crowd rushed to the lower mill and seized another man named Hughes. In the meantime Mr J. E. Greaves and Mr Warren Roberts, as they were proceeding for luncheon to Plas Waenydd, noticed a crowd running so they turned back and arrived just in time to rescue the man out of the middle of the crowd. The man was down on

the ground. He was removed to a place of safety and attended to. The two men assaulted had been working the quarry when the others had ceased.[22]

The intimidation experienced by blacklegs and others who refused to conform to the will of the majority, and the psychological effect which this could have upon them, is illustrated by some of the case histories of patients who were sent to the asylum.

In April, 1875 a quarryman Thomas Morris from Bryniau, Bethesda, was admitted.[23] On the commital papers certifying him for admission it stated that he was "Inattentive to his duties – also under the impression that his neighbours and fellow workmen are against him and saying that he is anxious to go to his father, sister and children who are dead. His wife testified that he had been getting up at midnight, under the impression that his fellow workmen will take him away and sacrifice him. A neighbour, Owen Thomas, had found him by the Felin Fawr reservoir, praying and saying that he was giving up his wife and children to the Lord and that his spirit would soon follow them; he was attempting to commit suicide. And another of his acquaintances, Thomas Jones, Penyffridd, had witnessed him attempting to cut his throat with a scissors. The certificate was signed by Hugh Hughes, Ogwen Terrace, Bethesda. The form also tells us other information about Thomas Morris; that he had nine children of whom six were still living, the youngest of them being seven years old. His bodily health had previously been very good, the doctor stating that he had not lost a day's work for many years. His disposition was described as sober and industrious, and he was a deacon with the Wesleyans. On his arrival at the hospital the asylum doctor was obviously concerned to establish whether or not these feelings of persecution were delusions. He clearly decided that they were not. The doctor wrote these notes on the patient's case record:

> He exhibited symptoms of insanity for the first time six months ago. The Penrhyn quarrymen were on strike but he was one of the few who kept on working – and being greatly annoyed by the former – it preyed on his mind and produced these attacks. On admission he was extremely low and unhappy – moaning and shedding tears but perfectly rational and well aware of his condition. He said that his mind had given way and that everybody, as he thought, were conspiring against him and that he was now being punished for his sins. No delusions.

[21] cited in Ieuan Gwynedd Jones, "The People's Health in Mid-Victorian Wales" in *Mid-Victorian Wales: The Observers and the Observed* (Cardiff, University of Wales Press, 1992) pp. 48–9, 176n.
[22] *North Wales Chronicle*, 8 July 1893, p. 8, col. a.
[23] DRO HD/1/360, Case no. 2441, date of admission 16 April 1875.

On admittance Morris was rather thin, and so he was given quinine to improve his appetite and a draught of chloral to help him sleep, and at the end of a fortnight he was beginning to improve. On 4 May the doctor made the following entry:

> Has continued steadily to improve. He acknowledges that he has been greatly benefitted here and that it has been the means of saving his life. Was today visited by his wife and son. Is perfectly rational in his conversation and with regard to his discharge says that he will submit to the decision of the doctor.

Morris was discharged recovered in July. The fact that he was able to recognise his own illness was a key factor in securing his early discharge. It implied that behind his acute anxiety and suicidal tendencies, was a "rational" being.

In 1881 a 30 year old man from Bethesda, David Parry Jones, was sent to the asylum.[24] He had been refusing to attend his work, had not been sleeping, had been noisy and troublesome, and had assaulted his housekeeper so that she had been obliged to flee from the house in the middle of the night. Evidence was given by his uncle, John Wheldon, of Llwyn Celyn, Llanberis, who stated that he "refuses to work and goes from house to house in search of a wife". On the notes attached to the case were further details elicited from the relieving officer, and David Parry Jones' nephew. These stated that:

> At the election of 1874 he was the only Conservative among the Quarrymen and was generally disliked by them after which he became low spirited. Subsequently a liberal union was formed among them and he refused to join and was in consequence taunted by them. He took this seriously until 3 or 4 years ago when he became excited; and he has been alternately excited and depressed ever since. He believes that all his neighbours are his enemies though this is not true – now at any rate.

In the asylum he was found to be in rather poor health. The doctor's case note records that he "is reserved but answers questions rationally. Says that he came here for a wife and that it is very upsetting that he cannot get one." He was discharged the following year, and apparently returned to work, for he was still described as a quarryman when he was re-admitted to the hospital some eleven years later, after another violent episode, this time toward his niece. On this occasion he was not discharged and remained in the hospital for the rest of his days.

Social, political and religious influences permeate the case histories of the patients sent to the North Wales Asylum during the nineteenth century. Religious ideas and notions were particularly prevalent, religion being a dominant force in the communities which the hospital served. Biblical imagery was widespread and often exotic, with birds and creatures, as well as biblical figures such as Job, Lot, John the Baptist, featuring amongst the delusions of the insane. Patients burst into lengthy bouts of preaching, fell upon their knees in prayer, and often suffered lengthy torment under the belief that they were sinners, some believing that they were irredeemably lost for having committed the "unpardonable sin" for which there could be no forgiveness.

E.W., a slate quarryman from Rallt, Plas Meini, Ffestiniog was only twenty years of age when he was sent to the asylum, suffering from religious mania.[25] He was constantly muttering and praying that "the fools may be made wise" and going through gesticulations with his hands, and placing himself on his knees. He was described as "an intelligent looking lad with fair complexion and hair, and pale blue eyes." On his left side, about the angle of the eighth or ninth rib was the mark of an cicatrix, large and deep, caused, he said, by a fall in the quarry in which he had probably sustained a compound fracture of the rib, as this bone presented much thickening. In the hospital he desperately wanted to go home; he hoped he said to become a preacher. However he was found to be masturbating (which was regarded at the time as almost inevitably giving rise to insanity), and also to have suppurating joints; his big toe turned gangrenous and came off. Yet at the end of the following year he was discharged to the care of his family. This frequently happened. When the patient's family realised that the afflicted person was not going to be cured at the hospital, and that they would probably die, they preferred to take them home to allow them to spend the rest of their days in the company of their friends and relatives.

This patient was possibly suffering from tuberculosis. The incidence of tuberculosis was extremely high amongst the quarrying communities, partly the result of crowded housing conditions, poor diet, and the working conditions at the quarries. At the time a link was often made between the incidence of tuberculosis in certain families and the occurrence of insanity. Both were widely viewed as hereditary in origin until at least the turn of the century. The case notes often contain the comment that the patient came from "a very phthisical family". G.J., the forty year old wife of a quarryman living in Penrhyndeudraeth, was

---

[24] Denbigh Record Office HD/1/361, Case no. 3059, date of admission 5 February 1881.
[25] Denbigh Record Office HD/1/360, Case no. 2614, date of admission 30 September 1876.

believed to be suffering from a hereditary form of insanity, although the immediate "exciting cause" was believed to have been "Change of residence after living for a long time in one place." It was recorded in her case notes on admission that her paternal uncle had died in the asylum fifteen years previously, that her brother was low-spirited for a year, that her grandmother was "melancholic" and that her father and two sisters had died of consumption. She remained in the asylum for over fifteen years, finally dying of cancer in August 1897.[26]

Some 17% of the patients admitted to the asylum between 1875 and 1914 were aged sixty years and over. Men who had survived years of hard work as quarrymen, who had brought up their families, and lived a full life, could show signs of mental illness in their declining years, and spend their latter days in the asylum. In fact men were often referred to as "elderly" when in their fifties.

T.P., a fifty-seven year old slate quarryman, of Brynhyfryd, Llanberis, who had always been regarded as steady and industrious, had been found by a neighbour on the street late on the night prior to his committal, behaving in an extremely excited manner, and using violence to anyone who approached him. He was a widower, and the father of six children, five of whom were living, the youngest being sixteen years of age. Dr W. Lloyd Williams, of Bryngwyddfan, Llanberis, wrote on the medical certificate which consigned T.P. to the asylum:

> During the last fortnight, I have observed the patient to be unnaturally talkative, going about the streets from early morning till late at night, preaching as he calls it to crowds of people. His whole conversation is irrational and at times if contradicted particularly he threatens to strike with a stick.

In fact this man had experienced a stroke about a year previously, and had never been the same since, being described as "peevish and irritable". On examination in the asylum he was found to have hemiplegia on the right side, though his other organs were apparently healthy. He was very confused in his ideas, preaching and discussing all kinds of schemes, and although he appeared to realise where he was, it did not seem to interest him. He was very irritable and would strike at the slightest provocation. His memory was much impaired. It was the change in behaviour that frightened and alarmed people. His son testified to his father's behaviour being "unnatural", and he

said that he had become unmanageable. T.P. remained in the asylum for five years, until his death in 1900.[27]

Another quarryman, aged sixty-two years, D.G. from Talysarn, bore the scars of two serious accidents in his working life, one to his left foot and another to his skull. The doctor noted that on examination, the "Patient is a tall elderly man, bald head and short grey whiskers. There is an old scar on his cranium and two scars on his nose – the front part of his left foot was amputated 15 years ago for an injury." According to the local policeman, Daniel had occasional bouts of intemperance. When the certifying doctor filled out the required lunacy papers, he wrote: "This man states he is possessed of property which he does not possess and that he earns enormous wages – also states that he is going to make a railway round the world, he is constantly praying and preaching incoherently." His wife, Mary, had told that magistrates that " ...he goes into shops and orders various items that are not necessary in large quantities, such as gold watches and chains and that he threatens to strike her when opposing him."[28]

Obviously, when someone began to behave in ways such as this it could be an acute source of embarrassment to the whole family. According to the case notes he much resented being sent to the asylum, and denied any claim to possessing large wealth. His memory was rather poor – he could not work out how long he had been in the asylum, and he claimed that his age was seventy-nine. In fact confusion over age was quite common. Shortly afterwards, this man had some sort of a seizure, and became partly paralysed, and he finally died in the hospital in May 1905. The cause of death was put down as "Softening of the Brain".

Of course, problems such as dementia and other age-related illnesses are no respectors of occupation, class or status. In 1877 the wife of a quarry manager was admitted to the Denbigh asylum suffering from the effects of bereavement following the death of her husband, and also from dementia.[29] She had previously been sent to the workhouse. She died in the hospital in the January of 1879. And in 1895 Dr John William, former surgeon to the Penrhyn Quarry hospital, and authority on the health of the quarrymen, author of the pamphlet *Peryglon i Iechyd Y Chwarelwyr*, was admitted as a private patient to the asylum. This, unlike a pauper committal, required evidence from two separate medical authorities. Here is the evidence recorded by the second of the two certifying doctors, Dr Arthur Hughes of Barmouth:

---

[26] Denbigh Record Office HD/1/333, Case no. 3211, date of admission 14 December 1881.
[27] Denbigh Record Office HD/1/368, Case no. 4875, date of admission 14 March 1895.
[28] Denbigh Record Office HD/1/373 Case no. 6111, date of admission 15 December 1902.
[29] *Ibid.*, HD/1/360, Case no. 2692, date of admission 31 July 1877.

Incoherency, is under many delusions such as believing that he is at home in practice at Bethesda, that his two thighs are dislocated, that he goes out fishing and takes hundreds of trout daily. He has the appearance and habits of an insane person and cannot sustain unbroken conversation for any length of time.[30]

A few notes were added to his case history at the asylum, to the effect that:

This patient has been surgeon to the Penrhyn Quarries for many years. He married for the second time some years ago a woman many years his junior. Soon after this he is said to have become intemperate. He gave up his quarry practice some time since and was engaged in private practice until 9 weeks ago when he became insane. A month ago he went to live with his sister at Dolgelley but has steadily become worse.

In the hospital John William appears to have been totally disoriented and was "full of all sorts of delusions." In 1897 a case note records "Same in every way, as deluded as ever, owns Merionethshire a present from the Queen. Is having a palace and hospital built with about 1,000 beds and he is going to be the head surgeon. Has married the daughter of the Tsar of Russia, whom he has delivered of a child. A very jolly old fellow, in good health." The case notes tell us that he eat and slept well, and seemed perfectly content, although his delusions were "too numerous to mention". He finally died of pneumonia in 1909.

It would be misleading to suggest that all cases followed on from some bodily ailment, or injury, or arose from incapacity or old age. Sometimes the onset of insanity could be startling and unpredictable. Lewis Davies was lodging at the same address, 33 Glynllifon Street, Blaenau Ffestiniog, as Evan Williams, and testified that the latter went out at 12 o'clock noon, and seemed rather in an excited state, went on to the top of the Mountain close by, very suddenly undressed perfectly naked, and ran about for miles.[31] He was said to be continually talking incoherently about religious matters – he claimed that he had at last seen Satan, and was continually repeating this all day. On admission to the asylum, in January 1890, he was described as a strongly built, respectable-looking fellow, but on the first night he was violent and struggling and had

to be put in the padded room. He then quietened down, and over the next fortnight showed some improvement. But on 11 February, the case note records, he "unfortunately relapsed and is now in an acutely maniacal condition, and during the last 2 days has been confined to the padded room. Refuses all food – and have had to give it to him forcibly with teapot." He did however once again improve, and was finally discharged recovered in 1891.

Force-feeding of patients occurred fairly frequently, and was regarded within the hospital as an effective means of dealing with cases of self-starvation. There seems to have been no attempt during these years, either by the doctors or anyone else, to question its morality.

The behaviour of the insane is often colourful and dramatic, and some cases must certainly have made a dramatic impression on passing observers. In 1879 a slate quarry labourer from Penmachno, Richard Richards, was admitted to the asylum.[32] He had been out of work for three months but a fortnight previously had got a job. He was said to have over-exerted himself, and on the fifth day he drank a considerable quantity of whiskey, soon after which he had jumped out of bed shouting that he was murdered, and was taken to the police station, and after that he gradually became worse. It appears that he was taken to the workhouse, because it was there that the certifying doctor filled out the forms securing his transfer to the asylum:

Swearing. I have heard him saying that he will save us all from everlasting punishment. He was boring a hole in the wall pretending to be blasting. Shouting terribly all kinds of nonsense. I am a bull and that he was Joseph Thomas of Carno [a famous preacher of the time]. He was also climbing up the workhouse gate calling himself Jesus Christ.

Around the same time a thirty-five year old quarryman from Mynachlog in Ffestiniog began to act in strange ways, saying that he possessed large sums of money and demanding to search the neighbours' houses for it, at the same time blacking his face imagining himself to be a Christy minstrel.[33] He too was sent to the asylum.

In 1880 another quarryman from Ffestiniog fancied that he had wires going through his bowels, and that people were meditating him injury.[34] But the hospital doctor soon recognised the symptoms – the thick and

---

[30] DRO HD/1/368, Case no. 566, p. 122 (private patient), date of admission 23 April 1895.
[31] Denbigh Record Office HD/1/365, Case no. 4143, date of admission 11 January 1890.
[32] Denbigh Record Office HD/1/361, Case no. 2851, date of admission 11 February 1879.
[33] Denbigh Record Office HD/1/360, Case no. 2541, date of admission 13 March 1876.
[34] DRO HD/1/361 Case no. 3041, date of admission 9 December 1880.

drawling speech, and feeble and unsteady gait signified that he was suffering from General Paralysis of the Insane, the tertiary stage of syphilis, for which there was no cure. At the time the connection between General Paralysis and syphilis was not sufficiently understood, and the "supposed cause" of his illness was put down as "anxiety of mind".

All forms of mental illness were frightening to the relatives. But happily not all ended in tragedy. In fact about 35% of all patients committed to the hospital were discharged cured within twelve months, some in far less. In 1905 a twenty year old quarryman insisted that he saw the Holy Ghost in the form of smoke, changing to the shape of a dog; his manner, conduct and language were totally at variance with his usual habits.[35] He had always been a quiet, and steady young man until he began to take an active part in the Religious Revival meetings, when some change in his behaviour was noticed. Once in the asylum he rapidly improved and within a month he was discharged cured.

Finally, the case of Griffith John Griffiths, a twenty-six year old quarryman from Pentre, Llanllyfni, admitted to the asylum in 1878, in a feeble condition, and suffering from Acute Mania.[36] The evidence adduced on his committal certificate states: "Entire change of character. Loss of memory. Talks about deceitfulness of parents. Obscene language and wants women in his bed with him." He had apparently become strange in his manner and behaviour some four to six months ago, becoming low-spirited and sometimes not speaking for hours together. He did not work for a month, and then went to work for a fortnight but gave up in the same space of time. Now he was not so low spirited but had become noisy and abusive and it was said that he "rambles about shouting". On his arrival at the asylum it was noted that he was "slight and spare – eyes blue – pupils dilated – complexion pale – hair dark, slight moustache. He was talking and shouting in high spirits, and still wanting women." He was given plenty of sedatives and purged, and then allowed to feed himself up on plenty of food. His bodily health improved, and he became quieter, and grew stronger, but remained very simple and childish; and he was discharged in November of the same year. However in October 1881 he was once again committed to the asylum, after endeavouring "to throw several of his fellow-workmen to the Quarry, a depth of over one hundred

yards". The asylum doctor observed what appeared to be a slow degeneration of the brain, and the patient thereafter remained in the asylum until his death in 1906.[37]

The foregoing cases serve to illustrate the wide variety of symptoms, in terms of behavioural patterns, which could be perceived to constitute mental illness. They enable us to appreciate how such *ymosodiadau disymwth* ("disturbing attacks") would indeed cause *braw a chyni yn fynych* ("terror and anguish frequently"). It is easy to understand why such events are so rarely spoken of or written about by victims, families or associates. The records preserved at the archives in Ruthin enable us to re-explore this opaque area of history, and by naming, make familiar, and thus less strange and threatening to us all.

Our initial attempts to utilise the records of the North Wales Asylum assuredly validate two sets of contentions. Firstly, that of a group of scholars who have become explorers of the "underside of society", who contend that the investigation of the submerged, the outcast and the deviant impells us toward a fuller appreciation of the taken-for-granted aspects of the so-called "normal".[38] Secondly, that of C. Wright Mills "... that the biographies of men and women, the kinds of individuals they invariably become, cannot be understood without reference to the historical structures in which the milieux of their everyday life are organised." [39] Inscribed in most of the records of the hospital patients are clues to domestic relationships and normative patterns in communities. Those of individuals from some distinctive occupational groups potentially provide much more, as we begin to chart their very direct linkages to capitalist enterprise, to trade cycles and to collective responses to economic exploitation. The detailed case notes of the North Wales Lunatic Asylum provide a series of unique portraits of individuals in distress and give some indication of the impact of their illness on their families and on the communities of which they were part. In particular the records relating to the quarrymen throw light upon the harsh conditions of their existence, and on the physical and psychological strains of their work. Indeed, the reading of their cases prompted one North Wales medical practitioner to remark "It is surprising that there were not more cases of mental illness, considering the *environmental* as well as the economic pressures which the quarrymen suffered."[40]

35 Denbigh Record Office HD/1/374, Case no. 6531, date of admission 7 March 1905.
36 Denbigh Record Office HD/1/360, Case no. 2769, date of admission 8 May 1878.
37 Denbigh Record Office HD/1/361, date of admission 25 October 1881.
38 Most notably Erving Goffman and Richard Cobb, and many students of deviancy from Durkheim onwards.
39 C. W. Mills, *The Sociological Imagination* (New York; OUP, 1968).
40 Dr Eddie Davies, Cerrig y Drudion, letter dated 13 December 1997 ("Mae'n syndod nad oedd mwy o afiechyd meddwl o ystyried y pwysedd *amgylchfodol* yn ogystal ag economaidd, yr oeddynt yn eu dioddef.") I should like to acknowledge the valuable assistance of Dr Eddie Davies in helping to decipher and interpret some of the medical case notes.

Book Reviews

Stephen Kotkin, *Magnetic Mountain: Stalinism as a Civilisation* University of California Press 1995.
ISBN 0-520-06908-0, 639pp.

Forty miles east of the southern tip of the Ural mountains is found the richest and most accessible iron ore in the world, in the *Magnitaia Gora*, the "magnetic mountain", so called because travellers found that their compasses behaved oddly once they reached this desolate place. It was at the fourteenth party congress in 1925 that the Bolshevik leadership resolved to transform this barren wilderness into a showcase Soviet industrial development. The first assault was mounted in 1929, when the initial detachment of workers arrived on horseback to begin the construction of a community that was to number 200,000 people. The plant itself was beyond Soviet resources to plan and build, so they accepted a tender from the capitalist West – from the Chicago firm of Freyn, between whose employees and the Soviets there was to be constant tension. Capacity was set at 2,500,000 tons a year, though the original blast furnaces were constantly breaking down, as Soviet workers, anxious to come up with results, worked too fast and inaccurately.

Even so, the results were impressive – 100 square kilometres of industrial territory was established, even if initially the steelworks was surrounded by mud huts that lacked a sewage system and a clean water supply, little different from the rural settlements of Tsarist days – indeed, one of them seems to have supported a church. Bit by bit a Bolshevik city arose, whose gleaming blocks of flats designed by the Frankfurt architect Ernst May were dominated by the headquarters of the local Communist party. For the managers and their families there was the élite settlement of Berezka some little way away. The newly-arrived workers could flock to the Magnitogorsk cinema to watch Hollywood talkies, either dubbed or in continuous translation, as well as home-grown thrillers such as *Party Card*, or could avail themselves of more lubricious entertainments on offer in a sleazy district known as Shanghai.

Kotkin traces the terrible privations endured by the first generation of Magnitogorsk residents and also the development and frenzied climax to the purges as they affected the new city, when different cadres denounced each other with ever more absurd accusations, arguing that the terror arose out of conflict between the Party and the NKVD. Despite the fear and suspicion, Kotkin makes it clear that this new Stalinist economy came into being because many thousands of ordinary Soviet citizens wanted it to happen, and were proud of their role in creating a new society. He quotes a letter from Anna Kovaleva, wife of a shunting locomotive driver who had won acclaim as a shock worker, to Marfa Gudzia, whose husband drove the dirtiest and most inefficient locomotive on the steelworks:

> Among such shock workers is my husband, Aleksandr Panteelevich Kovalev ... my husband trains locomotive drivers' helpers out of unskilled labourers. He takes other locomotive drivers under his wing. My husband receives prizes virtually every month ... And I too have won many awards. I will ask my Aleksandr Panteelevich to take your husband in tow, help him improve himself and become a shock worker, earn more. I want you, Marfa, and Iakov Stepanovich to be honoured and respected as we are, so that you live as well as we do.

Unfortunately Marfa was unable to read, and her husband is unlikely to have benefitted from Anna Kovelava's well-meant offer.

Kotkin's brilliant, readable, often highly entertaining, account sheds welcome light on a murky episode of Russian past which is now disgorging its archives in the wake of *glasnost* and the collapse of communism. It is, of course, far more than a contribution to the debate about the nature of the workplace and the social and economic imperatives which govern it, and in fact there is much more here about the way in which recreation and living conditions dictated the *mores* of the citizens of Magnitigorsk than there is about what went on in the steelworks themselves and how that affected people's lives. To utter a carping criticism, a weakness of this remarkable book is that it fails to consider work-patterns and work-processes in much detail, even though there is much on the men who ran the workplace. Yet as an account of the birth-pangs of a wholly new type of industrial community, one which, moreover, enabled the USSR to resist Hitler's guns, it could hardly be bettered; Magnitogorsk's bizarre echoes of the capitalist workplace that the Stakhanovites and the party cadres believed they were fast outgrowing makes the reader pause to consider how similar might have been the outlook of the denizens of the first generation of iron towns in Wales, of Merthyr and Blaenavon.

Peter Crew, Chris Musson, *Snowdonia from the Air: Patterns in the Landscape – Eryri o'r Awyr: Patrymau yn y Tirlun* (Snowdonia National Park Authority, Penrhyndeudraeth, Royal Commission on Ancient and Historic Monuments of Wales, Aberystwyth, 1996)

ISBN 0 948 16107 8, softback 56 pp, £9.95

This volume contains a number of impressive aerial views of sites of interest to the industrial archaeology and to the landscape historian and accompanying texts. Particularly interesting is the view of the Egryn and Hafotty manganese workings above Barmouth, insignificant extractions viewed from the ground, but an impressive landscape feature extending for several miles from an aerial perspective. Cefn Coch gold mine and Rhiwbach and Rhosydd slate quarries are represented by modern colour views, Graiglwyd and Dinorwic by black and white photographs taken by the R.A.F. in 1948 and by the University of Cambridge team in 1949 respectively.

* * * *

Dewi W. Thomas, *Hydro-Electricity in North West Wales* (Gwasg Carreg Gwalch, 1997)

ISBN 0 86381 455 7, softback 120pp, no price.

A comprehensive account of hydro-electrical development in the area, written by a former station manager at Dolgarrog. As well as the larger undertakings constructed by the North Wales Power and Traction Company, the C.E.G.B. and their successors, the author considers the pioneering efforts of Richard Edwards and Thomas Osborne Yale, and, of course, Moses Kellow. The only complaint must be the very poor quality of the photographic reproduction.

* * * *

C. J. Williams, *Metal Mines of North Wales: a collection of pictures* (Wrexham: Bridge Books, 1997)

ISBN 1-872424-58-9, 105 plates, no price given.

More than a re-issue of Chris Williams' earlier book, this attractive volume includes a number of new illustrations – for instance, Warington Smyth's painting of Hendre mine, Rhydymwyn, and photographs of reconstructed features at Minera – though Gutch's 1857 view of the ore-boats at Llandudno appear to have been published back to front. A useful book, which packs a lot of information in between its covers.

Edward A. Wade, *The Plynlimon and Hafan Tramway* Twelveheads Press 1997

ISBN 0 906294 38 X, hardback 72pp, £14.95

This book has been re-published to coincide with the centenary of the opening of the Plynlimon and Hafan Tramway. Although it lasted a mere two years, this narrow gauge railway has a fascinating history, touching on such areas as financial investment in rural west Wales, the speculative mineral and ore extraction industries of the nineteenth century, and the operation of an industrial and passenger railway. Ted Wade provides an interesting and very enjoyable insight into the archaeology of the railway, its history from its conception to its demise, and a detailed account of much of its engines and rolling stock. The book is well-illustrated with photographs (including evocative images of a special excursion into the bleak Cardiganshire landscape with passengers standing beside the railway's one carriage) and Ted Wade's own excellent scale drawings of the locomotives, including the bizarre *Victoria*, an 0-4-0 vertical boiler engine.

* * * *

Peter Johnson, *Ffestiniog Railway: A View from the Past* (Ian Allen, 1997)

ISBN 0-7110- 2512-6, hardback 112pp, £14.99

At last, a book of railway photographs that asks the question not only what do the photographs tell us about technical developments, but why were they taken in the first place, and what did they set out to show? The FR has always had a talent for publicity, so it is not suprising that as early as 1871, when *Little Wonder* was performing on Creuau Bank, John Owen of Newtown should have been paid to provide a photographic record of her efforts. R. H. Bleasedale of Alston, Birmingham was also probably commissioned by the Railway, though John Thomas, the Liverpool-Welsh photographer, made his way to Blaenau Ffestiniog as a freelance. In many ways his photographs are the most satisfying; railway enthusiasts often bemoan the driver and fireman who posed with their locomotive, thereby obscuring vital details such as a worksplate – true, but enginemen were a literally vital part of the railway scene, and John Thomas gives them pride of place, standing proudly on their machines, just as he recorded other men and women from both the old and the new Wales, the ballad-singers, quarrymen, dissenting ministers.

Since the history of the F.R. is so well known, there is no reason why this book might not have said less about the railway itself and more about the process of commissioning photographs, or the interest in railway scenes which photographers like John Thomas were able to exploit. Furthermore, though the story is followed up to the late 1930s, it only begins in 1871, and it might have been worth saying something of the prints of the railway in horse days.

* * * *

F. Ron Williams, *Llandudno and the Mostyn Influence* (Mostyn Estate and Llandudno and District Historical Society, 1996)

ISBN 1 898202 06 0, softback viii + 104pp, £7.95

Few communities in Wales have undergone more dramatic changes than Llandudno, until the 1850s a remote area given over to copper mining and sea-fishing, which suddenly metamorphosed into a holiday resort served by a main-line railway, the whole process initiated by, and under the strict control of, the Mostyn estate. This account, by a native of Llandudno, concentrates on the development of the estate from the enclosure award of 1843 to 1861, and provides a detailed and comprehensive description of the resort's early years.

* * * *

Anthony Jones, *Welsh Chapels* (Alan Sutton Publishing, Stroud, in Association with National Museums and Galleries of Wales, 1996)

ISBN 0 7509 1162 X, softback xiv + 146pp, £8.99

This volume is a substantial enlargement of a booklet originally produced by Dr Jones in 1984, and forms an invaluable introduction to what is surely the most distinctively Welsh form of architecture. It traces the story from the earliest temples of dissent to the few chapels built in Wales after the first world war. Long dismissed as ugly, derivative and lifeless, the Welsh nonconformist chapel is only now, as congregations dwindle and structures are demolished, receiving the scholarly attention it deserves. Pompous facades there are a-plenty in this book, but very many are graceful and attractive buildings, whose largely self-taught designers were increasingly aware of polite terms of architectural reference but did not allow their imaginations to be curbed by them. Dr Jones' enthusiastic advocacy provides an architectural counterpart to the debate on the nature of, and relationship between, the naive and the polite which Peter Lord's work has recently focused in Welsh visual culture. This has come none too soon; a comparison with the list of chapels to be "saved at all costs" published in the 1984 booklet makes depressing reading – within thirteen years Siloam in Bethesda has gone, as has Baladeulyn in Nantlle – though the statement in the present volume that Jerusalem in Bethesda is no

more will come as a surprise to last Sunday's congregation. Even so, the losses have been grievous and many, and it is much to be hoped that this book will help alert local authorities and others to the magnificent architectural legacy of these buildings, and their importance as components of Welsh townscapes.

* * * *

M. C. Reed *The London and North Western Railway* (Atlantic, Penryn, 1996)

ISBN 0 906899 66 4, hardback 248pp, £24.95

This history of the LNWR represents in many respects a return to classic railway history, focusing on events in the boardroom rather than on the footplate or in the signal box – as the author points out, much excellent work has recently been published on the technical history of the Premier Line. While there is little that is new on the subject of railway development within North West Wales, the importance of the local economy to the company is made clear. A number of the illustrations are of particular interest, in particular a good clear copy of the photograph of the mouth of the Blaenau Ffestiniog tunnel which was reproduced in Ernest Jones' *Blaenau Ffestiniog in Old Picture Postcards* (Zaltbommel 1985), which shows the contractor's saddle tank and the original Blaenau station. Others are John Thomas' photograph of the station staff and a light engine at Pen y Groes, and one of the experimental railcar that ran on the Nantlle branch.

SHORTER NOTICES

Geoff Price, *A nostalgic look at Llandudno and Colwyn Bay Trams since 1945* (Silver Link Publishing Ltd., Peterborough 1997)

ISBN 1 85794 094 6, hardback 132pp, £19.95

An attractive account of the latter years of this 3' 6" system, part urban tramway, part light railway, which closed in 1956. Terry Jones of *Monty Python* fame provides the foreword.

John H. Andrews *The Pwllheli & Llanbedrog Tramways* (D. Brown and Sons Ltd, Cowbridge 1995)

ISBN 872808 40 9, hardback, no price given.

An account of the passenger horse tramways of the Pwllheli area by the great-grandson of Solomon Andrews, the entrepreneur who developed the area as a resort.

Elfyn Scourfield, *Ceffylau Dur: Hen Beiriannau Amaethyddol* (Gwasg Carreg Gwalch, Llyfrau Llafar Gwlad, 1996)

RhLlSRh 0 86381 376 3, 70 tt, £3.75

Un o gyfres Llyfrau Llafar Gwlad, y mae'r llyfryn hwn yn disgreifio y ffowndrïau a gwneuthurwyr eraill peiriannau amaethyddol sydd wedi hen ddiflannu – fel y Brodyr Turner yn y Drenewydd, a gwnaeth byrddau llifio i'r chwareli hefyd, a Cudworth and Johnson.

Acknowledgements/ Cydnabyddiaethau

The editorial committee gratefully acknowledge the help and assistance from various sources; to David Longley, Director of the Gwynedd Archaeological Trust, for his advice and encouragement, and to the Trust's drawing office staff; to the Festiniog Railway Heritage Group newsletter, to Andrew Neale of Plateway Press and to Octel of Amlwch for their generous financial support.

Notes for contributors/ nodiadau i gyfrannwyr

Contributions should be sent to the editor, 2 Bryn Meurig, Tal y Sarn, Pen y Groes, Caernarfon, Gwynedd, LL54 6HW. They may be of any length, though it is difficult to find room for articles over 7,000 words. The editor cannot be responsible for the text of submissions. If at all possible, they should be on 3½" disc. The system we use is Microsoft Word, and the font is Times New Roman in 12-point (10 point for quotations separate from the main body of text). An initial summary of the article for inclusion as part of the published text is helpful, and Welsh-language articles should be followed by a brief outline of their contents in English.

Structure

If you wish to title sections and number sub-sections, rather than use continuous prose, the form we use is as follows (example taken from vol. one, article on Penscoins incline):

The Unloading Shed, Drumhouse and Incline
(i.e. in bold)
The drumhouse and unloading shed have been ...

1. THE UNLOADING SHED
The unloading shed is a rectangular building ...

(A) tip area
In the north-east corner of the building is a small tip ...
Further subdivisions of (A) may be indicated by lower case roman numbers within brackets, immediately followed by text, thus:
(i)

Style

Spelling: to follow *Concise Oxford Dictionary of Current English* or *Y Geiriadur Mawr.*

Quotations: to be enclosed within double inverted commas, quotations within quotations to be enclosed within single inverted commas.

References: wherever appropriate, sources should be referenced. The journal uses footnotes rather than endnotes or the Harvard system of author-date reference within the text. Typescripts

submitted can, of course, be adapted by the editor if your computer system does not enable you to do this. A **printed source** should appear thus in a footnote:

> [1] Sir John Wynne, *History of the Gwydir Family and Memoirs,* ed. J.Gwynfor Jones (Llandysyl, 1990), *passim.*

Manuscript sources thus:

> [6] NLW 4983. *(followed by page or folio recto-verso reference where appropriate).*

Articles in journals thus:

> [9] Robert Williams, "Hunangofiant Chwarelwr", *Cymru* XIX, Awst 1900, t. 88.

(Note that in the case of Welsh-language references, dates and page reference should be in Welsh).

Newspapers thus:

> *North Wales Gazette,* 31 January 1811, p. 3, col. a.

Measurements: these may be given in metric or imperial lengths, as appropriate.

Numbers: figures should be used for measurements, *e.g.* 200 metres, but time and figures under 100 should be expressed in words, hyphenated thus: twenty-seven.

Dates: in the main body of the text these are given as in the footnote reference above, thus: 31 January 1811.

Illustrations: maps, plans and diagrams to accompany articles are very welcome; contributors should note the page-size of the journal (10¾" x 8¼", 274mm x 210mm). They should be referred to in the text as (Fig. 1 *etc.*). The editorial board will gladly arrange assistance in the preparation of illustrations.

Photographs: these should ideally be black-and-white, and the caption should be marked on the back in soft pencil. This should include the call-number of those from libraries, archives, etc. They should be referred to in the text as (Plate 1 *etc.*).

For **book reviews,** information should be given in the following order: author, title, editor, publisher, place of publication, date of publication, number of volumes, number of pages, whether illustrated, ISBN number, whether hardback or softback or both, and the price, thus:

> Thomas Pennant, *A Tour in Wales,* ed. R. Paul Evans (Bridge Books, Wrexham, 1991) 2 vols., 1083pp., illustrations. ISBN for 2 vol. set, 1-872424-14-7, ISBN for vol. 1, 1-872424-15-5, hardback, 1083 pp. £45.

This example has been chosen as the most complicated; in practice few books have both an author and an editor, or have two ISBN numbers.

Any contributor who wishes guidance is welcome to contact the editor, 2 Bryn Meurig, Tal y Sarn, Pen y Groes, Caernarfon, Gwynedd, LL54 6HW.

Plate 17 *A group of three Dinorwic quarrymen around the turn of the century, taken by Griffith Jones of Port Dinorwic.*

Courtesy The Revd Michael Outram.